The Future-Ready
Organization

The Future-Ready
Organization

How Dynamic Capability Management Is
Reshaping the Modern Workplace

Gyan Nagpal

HARPER
BUSINESS

An Imprint of HarperCollins Publishers

First published in India in 2019 by Harper Business
An imprint of HarperCollins Publishers
A-75, Sector 57, Noida, Uttar Pradesh 201301, India
www.harpercollins.co.in

2 4 6 8 10 9 7 5 3 1

P-ISBN: 978-93-5357-009-5
E-ISBN: 978-93-5357-010-1

The views and opinions expressed in this book
are the author's own and the facts are as reported by him,
and the publishers are not in any way liable for the same.

Gyan Nagpal asserts the moral right
to be identified as the author of this work.

Typeset in 11/15.2 Aldine401 BT at
Manipal Digital Systems, Manipal

Printed and bound at
Thomson Press (India) Ltd

MIX
Paper
FSC FSC® C010615

This book is produced from independently certified FSC® paper to ensure
responsible forest management.

For Vir and Shyna

For inspiring me daily, through your resilience and your kindness.
You convince me that the next generation is indeed 'woke'.

CONTENTS

INTRODUCTION

'Transformation' must be the most worn-out word in business today. Beloved to the gurus, experts and consultants alike, transformations are often bandied around boardrooms as the magic pill to any number of organization maladies. Yet, while gladly swallowing the pill, many executives somehow miss the innate essence of the word even though the fundamentals of transformations can be observed all around us in nature.

Pause long enough to observe a grubby caterpillar become a majestic butterfly, a billion green leaves turn burnt-orange in autumn, or an ugly duckling develop into a beautiful swan, and it is difficult not to see the tragic brilliance within each of these makeovers.

They are all lessons in 'letting go'. Of losing everything you identify with first, before allowing a new identity to emerge from the remnants of an old one. Human greatness often comes from similar transformations. Buddha achieved enlightenment only when he gave up being a prince. Mahatma Gandhi went from wearing the tailored suits of a barrister educated in London to an ascetic who spun his own cotton to make cloth, exhibiting

1

through his own transformation the potent power of non-violent disobedience in the face of tyranny.

Transformations cannot happen on the margins and safe spaces, in functional agendas and underperforming pockets of the organization. They happen at the heart of every business. A business can't truly transform into a future-ready organization until it examines every assumption made and consciously questions the status quo. For example, should we continue to represent our organization's structure as a pyramid? Or who, in our vast and intricate network of relationships, creates true value for our customers? Who are our emerging competitors and why do they look radically different? Or should we continue to define our talent as the valuable few or focus instead on the limitless many?

These are both urgent and important questions to answer because as the evidence in this book will show, we can no longer grow in a reflection of our past selves. It isn't without reason that half the companies that occupied the hallowed Fortune 500 list in the year 2000 have now disappeared from the list.

The answers, this time around, won't come from experts, silver bullets and magic pills. *The world is moving so fast that we have few true experts on tomorrow. All we have are experts on yesterday.* The answers must come instead from deep diagnosis and purposeful experimentation. This book will help you to do both. It will help you update the lens through which your organization perceives its history, current reality and future opportunity.

Written with an eye on the digital horizon, the first half of this book presents an opportunity to step back and observe how both sources and patterns of organizational capability are evolving. The second half then lays out tools and frameworks which can help you map and manage the talent recipe at the heart of your business. The goal here is to make informed choices and build a future-ready talent system, powered by dynamic capability because as Heraclitus, the Greek philosopher, once said, 'Day by day, what you choose, what you think and what you do is who you become.'

And this is how we build future-ready organizations.

1

WHAT IS TALENT?

Invisible threads are the strongest ties.

–*Friedrich Nietzsche*

FOUR TALENT STORIES TO GET US STARTED

2001

The dot-com bust of 2001 mercilessly and rather indiscriminately shattered thousands of fledgling dreams in its wake. It was a financial hurricane blowing away digital castles built online from bits and bytes and data. The personal impact was brutal too. Starry-eyed entrepreneurs went from visions of changing the world in a hurry to the ignominy of a hard lesson learnt publicly.

Among these multitudes was 31-year-old Tony Fadell. A brilliant engineer, music fan and amateur disk jockey, Fadell had been forced to pull the shutters down on what had been a promising consumer electronics start-up. He had simply run out of cash. Limping stock markets, ravaged by failing internet stock, had dried up all sources of new funding. So much so that it was

5

probably easier to find a dehumidifier in the Atacama at that time than a chequebook on a technology investor.

Bruised but not broken and with belief in his concepts intact, Fadell put on a consultant's jacket and approached Steve Jobs at the newly resurgent Apple computers with a hot idea he had—of a hand-held music device capable of putting a thousand songs in your pocket.

Jobs, himself into his second stint in charge of a company he started in a garage, had just successfully revitalized Apple's core Mac computer business. His company—now back from the proverbial brink—had recently launched its revolutionary new X operating system, which included an exciting new music library feature, 'iTunes'.[1]

Jobs was betting that the iTunes software would go on to dominate the budding digital music industry, at a time when interest in digital music was rapidly rising as proved by the irreverent success of peer-to-peer sites like Napster. Jobs knew that if Apple didn't move fast, it would lose out heavily to Sony, the consumer electronics giant who was also investing heavily in online music technologies.

Impressed by Fadell as a person, Jobs instinctively liked the young inventor's idea of a rechargeable, hard-drive-based music player. A small, portable, digital 'jukebox', fully integrated with iTunes, could potentially change the music business for ever. So, in February 2001, Jobs offered Fadell a six-week consulting contract to develop an early prototype.

The first iPod—a perfect blend of Fadell's ideas, coupled with Apple's proficiency in software and design hit the shelves nine months later. With a 5-gigabyte hard drive, the revolutionary scroll wheel, an intuitive user operation and most importantly, seamless integration with the iTunes software, the first iPod was an instant success. Apple would go on to sell 400 million of them.[2]

1997

Fuki Sushi is a popular restaurant in Palo Alto, California. A regular haunt for sushi-loving Silicon Valley technology troopers, it just happened to be the venue for—what is now—a legendary 1997 meeting. One which would change the technology industry, and perhaps even the world, for ever.

Joe Kraus and Graham Spencer, Stanford alumni and the founders of Excite, a heavy-hitting internet search engine at that time, were at Fuki Sushi to meet a couple of geeky doctoral students from their alma mater. The meeting's focus was a radical new web search methodology built by the two students—PageRank.

PageRank was a search algorithm which graded and classified web content based on the quality of a web page's connections to other content. This wasn't just an innovative approach, it was a downright radical idea at that time, mainly because it differed considerably from the search industry's existing—and almost ubiquitous—standard of using keywords to help users search for content.

The students believed that the concept of academic citations was a superior representative of the quality of web content, as opposed to keywords. They argued that content which linked to more pages could be deemed better, hence it would command a better PageRank and should feature higher on search results. They had even built a prototype search engine called BackRub which demonstrated how the PageRank algorithm worked.

The two students knew that BackRub had the potential to qualitatively catalogue the nascent world-wide-web and grow with it. But with unfinished PhDs, they both saw the entire project as a temporary distraction from their doctoral studies. Selling it, hence, was the logical step.

The Excite team, intrigued, decided to run a few assessment searches on BackRub and compare the results with what their own search engine produced. It turned out that BackRub was much better. In fact, it was a little too good because it linked users to exactly what they were looking for, causing them to immediately move from the search page and click the search results. This was great for users but made little sense to search companies in an industry which was monetized for 'stickiness,' that is, an advertising revenue model designed to keep users on the home site for as long as possible.

Buying the technology would have cost Kraus and Spencer roughly 1.6 million dollars, with a chunk of it going to Stanford University which held the patent for the student project, and on whose servers Backrub ran. It was a great way to help their alma mater too.

In their wisdom, Kraus and Spencer decided to pass on the offer. The other big search engine at the time, AltaVista, had passed it too. Running out of options, the two students, Larry Page and Sergey Brin, decided to put their studies on hold, leave Stanford and incorporate a company to launch Backrub themselves. They named that company Google.

1976

With the Bee Gees and John Travolta fanning 'Disco Fever' across the globe, the spotlight was squarely off another, slightly nerdier teenage craze. Coin-operated arcade video games were taking America, Japan and other developed countries by storm. And at the eye of this storm was Atari's Arcade Pong, a megahit game. Pong had literally taken off like a rocket since it was launched on 29 November 1972.

By 1975, Atari was the undisputed 800-pound gorilla in the gaming industry, particularly after it scored a second superhit with Home Pong, a small, portable game console which took the addictive arcade game right into living rooms across America.[3]

Atari's co-founder, Nolan Bushnell, riding the wave of his company's meteoric success, was keen to take the embryonic electronic home gaming market even further. He placed his bets on the still-in-development-stage 'Video Computer System' or VCS—later called Atari 2600. The VCS was a modular system, with up to ten gaming options. With each game hosted on an independent cartridge, VCS could shrink an entire arcade into a tiny, portable box.

With all his energies invested in the VCS, sometime in 1976 Bushnell met an ex-employee, Steve Jobs, who wanted to pitch a product to him. Jobs had worked at Atari twice earlier. Once, just after dropping out from Reed College in 1973 and then more recently in 1975, when he worked on the printed circuit board design for the arcade game called Breakout.[4]

Bushnell, quite fond of Jobs, readily agreed to meet him along with Jobs's new business partner, Steve Wozniak. At the meeting, the duo showed Bushnell the computer they were designing and asked for urgent funding to scale up their garage project.

Jobs gave Bushnell two options—acquire a minority stake in the fledgling Apple Computers or the tempting choice to absorb their nascent start-up into Atari by buying the company outright.

Bushnell, with all his energies focused on video gaming, turned both the options down.

1975

Roughly a year before the Bushnell meeting, Steve Wozniak had designed his first computer—later to be christened the Apple I— while working at Hewlett-Packard.

An engineer in the scientific calculators division, 'Woz', as he was affectionately called, had worked on building his computer over countless weekends and most evenings after work.

In a 2013 lecture, Wozniak reminisced about those days, 'I was such a nerd coming out of high school that in those days I had little chance of having a girlfriend, or a wife. So, when I finished designing calculators at HP in the daytime, I went home, watched *Star Trek* and then (worked on his computer projects).'[5]

A conscientious employee, who didn't want to leave HP, Wozniak offered his designs to Hewlett-Packard. His reason for doing so was simple. As he had been a full-time employee of the company when he built the computer, Wozniak felt his current employers should have the first option to build it.

As Woz recollects, 'Five times they turned me down.'[6]

These are just four stories among many about unique, world-class talent. All four are relatively recent, uniquely independent, yet woven from a common thread. Each describes celebrated technologies which went on to change the world. And each chronicles key episodes in the history of the world's hottest technology companies today.

All four stories also demonstrate the relationship between brilliant individuals and remarkable organizations, validating why the 'art of business' is also the art of finding and retaining exceptional talent.

However, in each story, *this talent looks different*.

In the first one, Tony Fadell was a *consultant*. In the meeting with Nolan Bushnell, Steve Jobs was Atari *alumni*. Working long hours in a cubicle, Steve Wozniak was like any other *employee* walking the HP hallways at the time. And negotiating over Sushi were two *students*, Larry Page and Sergey Brin.[7]

Talent can sit anywhere, and *in a world more networked and connected than ever, your talent increasingly doesn't carry an employee ID*. In spite of this, most companies across the world continue to see talent management as an insular and inward-looking exercise.

They focus exclusively on an ever-shrinking pie of permanent headcount. This has got to change.

The Future-Ready Organization is an invitation to business leaders to step back and observe how established patterns of organizational capability are changing. By doing so, we will all begin to observe a new world of work emerging. In specific, we are entering an age where speed, flexibility, innovation and execution matter much more than decades-old qualifications or antiquated experiences dressing up a lengthy resume. This is also the time when some of the smartest people in business are eschewing the regimented rubrics of a nine-to-five job—or perhaps even the safety of a predictable and sequential career—in favour of more independence and self-direction.

In a business landscape fraught with disruptive and competitive forces, we are entering an age where smart organizations are adopting collaborative and partnership approaches to broaden their global impact. Collectively, these changes reframe the way we look at the true capability footprint of a business.

THE TIME IS RIGHT

In a 1992 commentary on the growing impact of what was then a fledgling knowledge economy, management guru Peter Drucker clairvoyantly wrote, 'Every few hundred years throughout Western history, a sharp transformation has occurred. In a matter of decades, society altogether rearranges itself—its worldview, its basic values, its social and political structures, its arts, its key institutions. Fifty years later, a new world exists. And the people born into that world cannot even imagine the world in which their grandparents lived and into which their own parents were born.'[8]

Drucker's fifty-year estimate sets the context for the disruptive shifts we observe all around us today. The knowledge economy isn't new, but it has only just started to mature. While digital commerce has been around, true digital disruption of whole industries has only just begun. Similarly, while the internet has become an integral part of our lives, the shift to device-based apps and cloud computing has only just begun to change the way we use it.

We are also rapidly approaching a critical tipping point within Drucker's half-century change cycle where several aspects of the way we live, learn and work will have to be redefined.

It is for exactly this reason that this book chooses to look at capability from the outside-in, rather than the other way around. We have spent decades looking at talent through a microscope, focusing narrowly on the talent we 'own' and meet every day within the boundaries of our factories and offices.

With significant changes on the horizon, it is time to trade in that microscope for a telescope—one on a pivot, like the ones found at tourist spots across the world—which allows us to see the entire landscape of capability surrounding our business. This telescope could help unlock tonnes of new ideas on how we could engineer future capability and competence for our greater economic good.

TALENT THROUGH THE MICROSCOPE

For the better part of forty years, human resource (HR) management practices have defined talent as a valued subset within an organization's employee base. And every arm of HR, therefore, has tried to maximize its unique contribution towards protecting and growing this subset. The hiring or talent acquisition practices, for example, are keenly calibrated for the hiring of 'like-for-like' skills whenever a position opens up in the organizational hierarchy. Other talent acquisition goals have focused on key demographics like college grads or diversity hires, which make the pipeline of promotable talent more robust over time. Most talent or succession management practices, for their part, continue to concentrate on just a few senior levels of the organization, aiming to build management bench-strength. Likewise, top talent development programmes invest disproportionate time and money in a chosen few—either a high potential group of future stars or a demographic subsection like women leaders, racially diverse management or expatriate talent.

These tactics aren't necessarily wrong. Each was an individually brilliant innovation in people management in its time. Yet, all the talent management practices described so far come from industry best practices in the 1980s and early 1990s. Moreover, they are all, without exception, inward-looking activities.

In the expanding and fast-paced world that is upon us today, it doesn't pay to be insular. With our microscope focused on just a select few, we risk missing the wood for the trees, like Nolan Bushnell did at Atari. In modern business, our inability to spot exceptional talent or exceptional ideas could prove suicidal. For proof, we don't need to go beyond the stories with which we started this chapter. Atari was struggling barely seven years after Bushnell declined Jobs's offer. And Excite was wiped out a few quarters after Google's advent in 1998.

Hence the need for greater outside-in thinking and outside-in talent management. This also forces us to step back and re-examine the fundamental management relationship between an organization's performance and its headcount. In other words, given the disruptive, technology-fuelled age we inhabit today, people management practices can no longer exist purely to squeeze out more performance from internal resources.

As a discipline, management must grow and adapt to mirror the evolution of modern business, as a whole. It must change with the times. A key change this book focuses on is how we perceive and engage human capability in the pursuit of organizational objectives.

Over the following chapters, this book will present compelling evidence which shows exactly why it serves the industry better to broaden the definition of an organization's talent beyond just those on the payrolls. *In a future-ready organization, 'talent' is increasingly a metaphor for 'capability'—at the right place, at the right time and equally, at the right price.* This capability can come from anywhere—full-time employees, part-time employees, contractors, consultants, strategic outsourcing, tactical insourcing, strategic partnerships, collaborations, mergers, acquisitions, joint ventures and increasingly, intelligent automation. Capability wears many badges today.

To take this interpretation one step further, I would also say that from a business leader's perspective, talent is *any capability which creates economic value* for an organization's customer or shareholder. This is the value proposition which must concern us. I find that more CEOs intuitively accept this new definition of talent. In my travels since my last book, I have had the opportunity to discuss this topic with leaders at a number of my client organizations or at CEO summits and roundtables where I often speak. Invariably, I find them in strong agreement. Most P&L accountable leaders are less concerned about headcounts and more interested in accessing the right capability, at the right time and in a manner which affords them strategic flexibility.

In conversation, CEOs today agree that the old days of 'binge hiring' for ever increasing headcount numbers are behind us. Their experiences with restructuring and strategic outsourcing since 1990 in particular have convinced many business leaders that the future invariably belongs to the lean yet interdependent, collaborative and networked enterprise.

However, for all their conviction and enthusiasm, many also feel a sense of anxiety at the growing chasm between the current pace of innovation or experimentation in management sciences and the administrative needs of future enterprise.

SWAPPING THE MICROSCOPE FOR THE TELESCOPE

I am more optimistic, purely because I see most organizations have already started recognizing that old tools aren't working. Some have even started experimenting, even if tactically so, whilst others—particularly those in new technology or start-up businesses—have intuitively adopted a newer age talent management philosophy as part of their core operating culture.

The issue, however, is one of perspective, particularly within companies which refuse to challenge outdated talent assumptions. Driven by a process-fuelled slumber, these organizations often shy away from seeking unfamiliar yet truly strategic insights into a rapidly evolving capability landscape. A good example of this strategic myopia can be found in a recent boardroom conversation I had:

CASE STUDY: YOUR CURRENT TALENT ECOSYSTEM

As talent strategists, my colleagues and I help several companies think through their future talent challenges. At one such organization, we were at a quarterly management review when the question of a recent hiring freeze came up. After the resultant moaning had died down, my interjection to the debate seemed innocuous enough, 'So hiring is clearly an issue. We know that. But this is a very successful business, and we have many sources of talent. Who can tell me—**what does your current talent recipe look like?**' Seeing their quizzical faces, I rephrased my question, 'Where do you currently source capability from?'

I saw all eyes shift and settle on the head of HR, an exceptionally smart and well-regarded executive, who shuffled through some papers before saying, 'We had 65,112 employees at the end of last month.' 'That's great,' was my response. It was a good start, but I was looking for more. 'Where else do we source capability from?' By then, several other executives in the room seemed to have caught on to my drift. 'We outsourced 600 jobs recently,' the CFO said, 'and we have seventeen priority vendor contracts.' 'We distribute through JVs in a few countries,' someone added, as others joined in too. As the conversation progressed, I noticed the CEO leaning forward in rapt attention. 'We don't have a grip on this, do we?' he finally concluded.

So, we agreed to pause the conversation and get some work done before the next review. In the weeks that followed, a cross-functional team cobbled together from finance, procurement and HR helped me draw up a more accurate capability map. We presented the chart in fig. 1.1 at the next quarterly review.

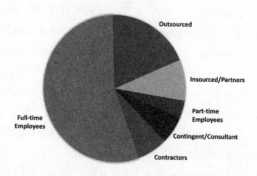

Fig. 1.1: The Organization's Talent Mix

The result surprised many in the room and the debate which ensued was rich and nuanced. The fact that full-time employees formed just 55 per cent of the current talent recipe was particularly hard to stomach. One executive shared that although a similar historical view didn't exist, the share of payroll employees would probably have been much larger five years ago. Others described the disparity which existed in how capability was sourced and governed. The head of HR reflected on how much time and effort went into onboarding and training employees, with almost nothing invested in other segments.

I barely spoke after the first ten minutes. And almost no facilitation was required over the next fifty. They were asking all the right questions themselves. It was now time to take them forward, that is, talk strategy. 'So this is your reality today,' I said. **'What will your talent recipe look like in five years?'**

I found true joy working with this executive team. In the months that followed, we managed to sustain a rich dialogue about how access to capability at an industry level was evolving and even put in place a cross-functional team of leaders to carry this debate forward.

A BROAD DEFINITION OF TALENT MAKES SENSE

In the conference speeches I give, I often like to play a little game with the audience. I flash a series of competing realities on screen and ask the audience to vote with their gut—and raised hands. The options I give them include a choice between *fixed* or *flexible*, *permanence* or *evolution, competence* or *innovation, sturdy* or *nimble,* etc. I've run this activity scores of times, in Western countries and Eastern ones, on both sides of the equator. In every room I have worked, I find the audience has raised more hands for latter options over the former.

These are smart men and women, with strong instincts. Business leaders are intuitively strong at spotting polarities and in recognizing in which direction the winds of change are blowing. This is exactly why, as I mentioned earlier, P&L leaders today care less about headcount and more about capability which creates economic value. This, hence, should be our new definition of talent.

This tilt reassures me immensely, as I believe it should be the P&L leaders (and not HR) who now occupy the vantage point from which to orchestrate talent strategy. They are in the best position to discover all possible sources of capability, both internal and external, or fixed and flexible. They are also in the best position to compose a unique and conscious talent recipe which serves the long-term business strategy.

Often, the talent with the greatest opportunity to create economic value for shareholders sits outside your organization. Tony Fadell's impact on Apple's long-term share price (see the opening case study) is a perfect example. Similarly, many times key talent with the opportunity to create an impact on customers does not possess an access card or an employee ID. One of the best examples from my recent experiences can be found in the next example.

CASE STUDY: THE HOTEL DRIVER

I live in the ultra-efficient city-state of Singapore, but with clients on three continents, my work week often begins with an international commute. Over the last fifty-two weeks, for example, I packed a bag twenty-nine times. Needless to add, I spend a fair number of nights in a hotel room. Like most business travellers, I have my favourite hotels, and in most cases, they aren't the most luxurious or expensive ones in the city. Actually, there are two things that help get a hotel on my favourites list more than anything else. The first is location and the second is efficiency.

On a typical business trip, I arrive at my destination airport and have a hotel transfer waiting for me. The car ride from the airport to the hotel averages anywhere between twenty and forty-five minutes depending on the time of day or night. Now, I like playing my little harmless games, as you have seen, and often with forty-five minutes to kill, these drives are the perfect opportunity for them.

My favourite activity while being driven to a hotel is to strike up a conversation with my chauffeur and find out who they work for. Most drivers, it turns out, aren't employees of the hotel I am staying at. Some work for car rental agencies, others for contractors who provide a fleet of cars to the hotel chain—making each individual driving my car into a 'contractor of a contractor'. Others are independent owners—freelancers or micro-entrepreneurs with a single car—who invariably have Uber-like arrangements with concierge desks at several hotels in the city. It's been years since I came across a driver who was a fixed, full-time employee of the hotel which hosted me.

Now let's contrast this with my experience at the hotel itself. On a normal two-night stay, I probably spend two minutes checking in, and I always wheel my own carry-on to the room. The only meal I have in the hotel is breakfast, where a server spends all of thirty seconds with me, pouring a cup of coffee, getting my room number on a check or clearing my plate. I never meet the housekeeper who cleans my room and I never call the operator—I trust my cellphone more at managing my morning alarms. At the end of the visit, the check-out takes another three minutes or so, before I walk out the door without as much as a thought of having *spent just five-and-a-half minutes interacting with employees and forty-five minutes with a contractor of a contractor.*

This experience has repeated several times over the last year. I'm sure those who travel frequently would also report something similar. I'm not saying that all the highly-trained employees working behind the scenes are delivering one-ninth the value a contractor is delivering. Not at all. On the contrary, hundreds of employees work tirelessly to ensure a million little details come together for a perfect hotel stay.

However, customer retention in a competitive and fast-paced industry like hospitality demands that organizations squeeze out as much value as possible from the little time they have with the customer. And hence, here's what I would like you to consider— on our drive in from the airport, if I ask the driver where within the hotel could I find a meal at 11.30 p.m., or if the hotel has 'coffee to go' available in the lobby each morning, what kind of answer do you think I normally get? In my experience, questions such as these often elicit a shrug or a non-committal response.

At a systemic level, this reflects a broken talent system—one where the hotel's HR team spends millions of dollars training employees to high levels of excellence in how to communicate with a customer, yet has zero time or interest to invest in the wider talent ecosystem, purely because of an industrial-era bias against contract staff.

Instead, it has now become every CEO's job as the chief talent strategist to ask three important questions. In this case, it is the hotel General Manager's task to gather her or his senior team and ask:

1. Who inhabits our current talent landscape? Who is creating value for our customers and other stakeholders?
2. How do we source and cultivate capability? And how does this challenge legacy assumptions or management practices?
3. What can we do to improve this recipe in the future? Where can we enhance capability, flexibility, efficiency or value?

As the answers to these questions emerge, so does your talent strategy. If there is one thing that these three questions collectively teach us, it is this:

In the modern, networked and symbiotic world we live in, people management is less about squeezing performance from the organized few and more about curating contribution from the limitless many.

DIGITAL DISRUPTION

There is an additional (fourth) question I believe every organization should be asking itself too. It is: 'How is the digital economy transforming our talent recipe?' And you may be surprised at how many changes are already in play.

The first step in answering this question is to map your current talent realities. Creating a 'current capability' pie chart, like the example in fig. 1.1 earlier in this chapter, is a great way to start. Especially if you aspire to become a future-ready organization, pull your talent management practices out of the industrial age and orient them to the knowledge age. And given the imminent and concurrent digital disruptions in many industries, you may just be running out of time.

A 2015 report by IMD and Cisco, covering 941 business leaders found that over 40 per cent of leaders in employment-heavy industries like manufacturing, hospitality, travel, retail, healthcare, banking and media, believe they could be put out of business by impending digital disruption. As the survey's authors noted, 'Digital disruption has the potential to overturn incumbents and reshape markets faster than perhaps any force in history.'[9]

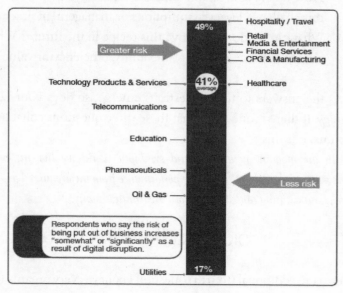

Source: Global Center for Digital Business Transformation, 2015
Fig 1.2: Industries at Risk

Currently, the industries at a 'greater risk' of disruption (fig. 1.2) collectively employ over a billion workers. When the survey team asked business leaders for an indicative timeframe when disruptive technologies would start to alter the balance of power within their industry, they found: 'The average time to disruption (meaning a "substantial change" in market share among incumbents) was 3.1 years, a dramatic escalation in the rate of competitive change versus historical levels.'

The payoffs from disruptive technologies can be huge. As recent evidence shows us, companies which embrace and drive digital innovations don't just survive. They wipe out the competition. McKinsey researchers who track this phenomenon say, 'Digitally-enabled innovations often have network effects associated with them, which in turn leads to "winner takes most" outcomes; the top performing companies enjoy far higher profit margins than the rest, and a handful of frontier firms are leaving everyone else in the dust.'[10]

For proof, all we need to do is look at what Google, Apple or Samsung are doing to the pack of companies chasing them.

It is easy to assume that all the disrupters are niche and nimble start-ups who have never known the old economy, but this is far from the truth. Several large industry leaders are successfully digitizing their entire business as you read this. Chinese electronics firm Haier is one such example, as is GE's deep investments in the industrial internet as well as DBS bank in Asia, which is embracing a digital future faster than any of its competitors. Even cities are joining the act, with smart cities like Singapore, Dubai or Zhenjiang (near Suzhou) in China investing billions in networking and data connectivity, promising residents everything from instant data on transport to real-time disaster management using smartphone applications.

Digital disruption promises to change business models and alter the fundamental architecture of jobs within every industry. And as the world of work changes, so do the capabilities which create value. What would work look like when tens of micro-jobs replace what is a single job today? Or when digital access finally supersedes physical access, turning work itself into an application on your device. In other words, imagine a day when employment status or even management hierarchy becomes a function of a unique password and the depth of access it provides. In such an environment, companies could theoretically have hundreds of digital employment packages on offer; a scenario which would finally and irrevocably flatten the world for global talent. What about the human cloud or recent advances in chat-bot technologies and artificial intelligence?

These trends—and more similar ones—are already practical realities in several industries. While in others, like driverless cars for example, they are close to or waiting for a large-scale technology tipping point. Together, these trends are changing the why, how, where, when and who of work as we know it today. In the subsequent chapters of this book, we aim to understand this new world, and equally, to craft a meaningful response.

2

HOW EMPLOYMENT CHANGED

Abundance is not something we acquire. It is something we tune into.

—*Wayne Dyer*

Building a future-ready organization involves getting leaders tuned into the art of the possible. Doing so allows them to see capability as a dynamic rather than a static construct. However, before we master the management of dynamic capability and define what talent in the future is, it is important to understand the journey which brought us here in the first place. In particular, how the social contract between an organization and its talent was cemented during the industrial age and why the employment monolith is crumbling today.

SCARCITY OR ABUNDANCE

Economics as a science is all about scarcity. For hundreds of years, microeconomics in particular has studied and theorized how market forces (demand and supply) are probably the most efficient means to distribute—and determine the relative value of—scarce resources.

In general terms, the scarcer a resource is the more valuable it becomes, either as a commodity to be put to further use or as a store of value. This broad description of scarcity has driven commerce for millennia, well before the first economist could ever assume that title. Think of gold, which has held its value since the time of ancient Egypt, or the overland silk route from China, which flourished for a thousand years, as well as the spice trade from India, fuelled by insatiable European demand for that magical condiment called pepper. The evidence clearly shows that it is scarcity, more than anything else, that drove civilizations to cross vast oceans to trade—or to conquer.

The economics of scarcity became more pronounced during the industrial age, on the back of the rapid commoditization of resources, which in turn caused an explosion in global trade for both raw material and finished goods. And while this was generally good for global prosperity, every silver cloud has a dark lining too. Every enterprise, no matter how big or small, now had to worry about short-term spikes or troughs in demand or supply of raw material and the resultant consequence of price volatility on their business.

The funny thing is that while economics has both a theory of scarcity and abundance, the former gets the lion's share of attention. There is a simple one-word reason for this—money, and how money has appropriated the concept of 'value.' This is so ingrained in our psyche and way of life that we struggle to spot the distinction between value and price.

Let me explain. Our obsession with scarcity makes us take for granted the very things that our survival depends on—air, water, climate, food, safety, relationships. I could go on and on. It's only when something critically important becomes scarce and hence expensive that the human mind begins to acknowledge its value.

Individuals fall into this trap, and so do institutions, mainly due to the industrial mindset which makes up modern business. However, in the knowledge age—and especially since the advent of the digital economy—it becomes imperative that we examine some of the core assumptions around scarcity and abundance.

While physical resources and manufactured goods might continue a unidimensional existence based on monetary value, several key ingredients of the knowledge economy don't necessarily follow suit.

The great Peter Drucker spotted this twenty years ago when he presciently observed how valuable the free flow of information was to the knowledge economy. As he re-emphasized in the 2001 masterpiece, the *Essential Drucker*, 'Then there is the new "basic resource" information. It differs radically from all other commodities in that it does not stand under the scarcity theorem. On the contrary, it stands under the abundance theorem. If I sell a thing—for example, a book—I no longer have the book. If I impart information, I still have it. And in fact, information becomes more valuable the more people have it.'[11]

Similarly, several other input factors which define success in the digital age, such as networks and communication, also increase in value as their abundance grows.

That is not to say that all resources powering the digital age are abundant. Several critical inputs, particularly those with a clearer monetary value in the near term, are subject to scarcity. Nonetheless, it is liberating to realize that several core management assumptions of the last century can be increasingly and successfully challenged. For it is in our assumptions that the future is won or lost.

Let's look at talent as an example. Most business leaders today rank talent as the scarcest commodity in business. I have lost count of how often I have heard a CEO or Head of HR say good people are hard to find. It is a classic scarcity trap. This refrain was especially loud in the three or four years preceding the global financial crisis in 2008 and continues to be a major issue in high-growth industries or markets today. I was so captivated by this notion of talent scarcity, when in reality our planet is in a historical talent sweet spot—in terms of both quantity and quality—that it prompted me to research and write my first book, *Talent Economics*,[12] in 2012.

Data tells us that we have 3.4 billion people of working age who wake up every morning looking to pursue an economic endeavour. Barely fifty years ago, this number was half what it is today. And fifty years, when seen in the context of human history, is like a blink of an eye. So, scarcity cannot be due to fewer numbers of people available.

We also have a record number of college graduates and postgraduates across the global talent system today. This number continues to grow. There are more engineers, more trained healthcare professionals and more management graduates than ever before. Workers are better educated, more qualified and highly trained too. Hence, it can't be the poor quality of talent which has got us in this situation. Workers today also have access to unprecedented technology and mechanization which make them faster and more productive. So, human efficiency is also not to blame.

Why then does consulting major PWC's sample of 1,344 business heads in 68 countries find an astounding 93 per cent dissatisfied with their current talent strategies?[13]

THE SOCIAL CONTRACT

To answer this question, we must examine our fundamental assumptions about 21st-century talent. Do we assume talent to be an individual, who is physically present at a specific place at a specific time? Or as we described in chapter one, do we assume it to be capability, which increasingly isn't confined by time and space?

By reframing this assumption, we take the concept of talent from a finite, limited and hence scarce commodity and transform it into a resource with great flexibility and abundance. Let's examine this assumption from two perspectives—physical location and time orientation.

1. *Location*: For hundreds of years, the concept of work has been inseparable from the individual who does it. With industrialization and the rise of white-collar work in the 20th century, this inseparability only became stronger. Over the last 120 years, this link has been epitomized by a social structure called the 'employment contract'. While the concept of a work contract has existed since Roman times (*locatio conduction operarum*), the current anatomy of the post-industrial employment contract emerged in the early 20th century from the ashes of the Masters and Servants Acts which had governed labour relations since the early 1800s. And they were a significant improvement. For one, they forced employers to specify the precise tasks that an individual was being hired to do and the location of those tasks, and articulate a price they were willing to pay for this body of work. It also committed both short and long-term benefits, gave employees the right to collective action and included provisions against unfair dismissal.

2. *Time*: Once signed, it was in the mutual interest of both parties to see the employment contract as a long-term arrangement. On the one hand, it helped the employee hedge against short and long-term financial risk, including

post-retirement income, while on the other, it helped the employer build a stable workforce which could mature in line with company growth.

We now know that this arrangement worked brilliantly in the West to fuel great prosperity through the latter half of the industrial age. The articulation of specific tasks helped schools and universities further professionalize academic curricula, thereby creating a steady stream of ready talent for employers—the MBA being a good example. The stability and structure that work provided also drove urbanization, as increasing numbers of rural families invested in college education or migrated to urban centres, looking for work.

In a nutshell, it was this growing pipeline of educated labour looking for contractual employment that catalyzed rapid industrialization across much of the developed world.

Yet, for all these great outcomes, the greatest benefits accrued not to the employer, but to the employee. A stable income, coupled with worker protection, short-term benefits like sick pay or vacation leave and the long term guarantee of a retirement income, led to huge upgrades in standards of living and consumption levels. The golden age of employment laid the foundations for the creation of vast middle classes on both sides of the Atlantic.

FROM THE BALANCE SHEET TO THE P&L ACCOUNT

Things started to go sour, though, as early as 1963, when the US car company Studebaker went into bankruptcy. This, in turn, resulted in the sudden and wholly unexpected collapse of its employee pension plan,[14] an event which shook the collective consciousness of the American workforce. With millions wondering if this could happen to them later in life, legislators were soon locked in a fresh debate on how best to hold companies to their long-term pension promises.

However, with corporate balance sheets now carrying billions of dollars of pension liabilities and threatening the future solvency of the company themselves, business executives had other ideas.

Chief Financial Officers across US and in other industrial powers spent much of the 1970s urging their boards to vote for policy shifts on pension liability. They wanted a transfer of long-term benefit costs from the balance sheet to the P&L account. In other words, rather than committing to provide post-retirement pensions to employees, companies would now pay out the benefit via a monthly or annual payment to a statutory or private pension fund. In the US, the government provided a possible solution via the employee-nominated 401(k) pension providers.

And boards listened to them. The evidence shows that guaranteed (defined benefit) pensions have been in a freefall since 1980. In the US, the number of employer-supported pension plans peaked at a high of 1,75,143 in 1984. In 2014, there were less than a quarter of that number left.[15]

At that time, expensing off pensions as a benefit seemed to be a victory for both parties. It seemed to make financial sense to both the employer and employee. Companies could reclaim their balance sheet while giving workers greater control over their long-term financial destiny. Employees could now (theoretically) choose from hundreds of private pension providers based on their specific investment horizon and risk appetite.

In hindsight, this irretrievably altered one of the fundamental tenets of the employment contract. It effectively passed the responsibility for long-term financial risk from the employer to the employee. Over the past forty odd years, with the increasing monetization and transferability of retirement benefits, one of the fundamental outcomes of employment—long-term financial security—is no longer a function of devotion to one employer. And the consequences of this shift have been huge—the virtual destruction of employment loyalty. Talent has discovered its legs.

Employees today can easily monetize their skills and seek better pay and benefits elsewhere. There is practically no financial disincentive to leaving a company.

Booming job mobility showed that the talent market began voting with their feet. As the individual—and individual alone—was now responsible for the long-term financial future of both self and family, the newly empowered employee had no credible incentive to suffer dead-end jobs or churlish supervisors.

By 1990, employers were already reeling from a devastating erosion in employee loyalty. Furthermore, it wasn't the marginal players or poor performers who were leaving. It was the best and brightest. By 1997, McKinsey and Co. had given this phenomenon a name. The 'war for talent' was here to stay.

The spike in employee mobility through the 1990s was a direct consequence of the monetization and portability of benefits. But it wasn't just the newly-mercenary employee who had changed.

Loyalty cuts both ways and significant changes were afoot on the employers' end too—changes that not only compounded the budding war for talent but fundamentally rewrote the century-old benevolent bond of kinship between an organization and its employees.

In the summer of 1990, the *Harvard Business Review* carried a seemingly routine management commentary by MIT computer science professor Michael Hammer titled 'Reengineering Work: Don't Automate, Obliterate'. The article was an attempt to show companies how exponential efficiency could be achieved through what Hammer called 'business process reengineering'. In essence, what he was asking companies to do was to consider redesigning entire processes using exciting breakthroughs in computing technology.

Hammer was particularly frustrated by the short-sighted ways in which companies were computerizing. It was a common sight in the 1990s to see companies buying hundreds of computers for managers and functional teams, purely to help them do existing work faster. Most users saw them as souped-up calculators or an evolved typewriter with memory, rather than breakthrough productivity devices. Hammer, for his part, didn't see computers as a way to speed up work, but rather as tools which could automate the work itself.

As Hammer explains, 'The usual methods for boosting performance—process rationalization and automation—haven't yielded the dramatic improvements companies need. In particular, heavy investments in information technology (IT) have delivered disappointing results—largely because companies tend to use technology to mechanize the old ways of doing business. They leave the existing processes intact and use computers simply to speed them up. But speeding up those processes cannot address their fundamental performance deficiencies. Many of our job designs, workflows, control mechanisms and organizational structures came of age in a different competitive environment and before the advent of the computer.'[16]

Through the rest of the article and his follow-on 1993 book with James Champy,[17] Hammer spoke of the exponential savings in time, cost and resources, which were possible by following his suggestions. Re-engineering, he promised, could lead to 'quantum leaps in performance' and benefit customers through better quality, consistency and faster service.

A brilliant mind and an astute strategist, Michael Hammer was onto something huge. Not only was he calling out a 'tipping point' at the very moment it tipped, he was also offering us a real roadmap over to the other side. Quite like Peter Drucker who—as we saw in the opening chapter—said famously, 'In a matter of decades, society altogether rearranges itself.'[18] Except that Hammer was going a step further. He was showing us what this rearrangement might look like too.

In practice, though, the thousands of management consultants, stock analysts, investment bankers and chief executives who ended up following his advice through the 1990s probably lacked the vision Hammer had for the world ahead. Re-engineering activity ended up being implemented less through fundamental process improvement and automation and more as buzzwords like rightsizing and restructuring. Hammer's work became less about value to the customer or the business and more about value to the shareholder.

YOU'VE BEEN RESTRUCTURED

Before the 1990s, lay-offs were an act of last resort. If a company was at a risk of going under and hence let workers go or shut a factory, those affected reluctantly recognized that the owners had no options left. The triggers of a forced layoff were mostly external.

The rapid rise of restructuring in the 1990s represented something entirely different. For one, the triggers were largely internal. And companies weren't restructuring only when survival was at stake. Often, it was the other way around. In 1996, for example, Applied Materials made record profits—and fired 10 per cent of its workforce.[19] Around the same time, AT&T also announced it was firing 40,000 workers or 13 per cent of its workforce, at a time when, as the *New York Times* reported, 'the company is healthy and when almost all segments of its business are profitable and growing'.[20]

These 'healthy restructures' weren't isolated surprises to their talent. Restructuring was spiking in almost every industry. Probably because stock markets loved them, assuming every downsizing announcement automatically implied a proactive management team, reduced long-term costs and the promise of profit-maximizing efficiencies. This short-term increase in share prices further emboldened Board members to justify the next round of restructuring activity, creating a self-fulfilling prophecy of sorts.

NEGATIVE RETURNS

Restructuring activity peaked during the 1990s, effectively transforming the pink-slip from a tool of last resort into a management device. But much of the re-engineering redundancies during the time ended up being cosmetic rearrangements and hardly transformative in nature. The gains were short lived too, because unless the workflows themselves are fundamentally redesigned or outsourced, growing companies tend to rapidly bloat headcount once again. Further, many of the headcount cuts achieved were often in junior and administrative levels, where marginal salary savings were smaller than at senior levels.

The financial gains from re-engineering were largely mythical too. In 2010, *Newsweek* published a damning indictment in which it wrote: 'An examination of 1,445 downsizing announcements between 1990 and 1998 also reported that downsizing had a negative effect on stock-market returns, and the negative effects were larger the greater the extent of the downsizing.'[21]

The negative stock returns proved to be just the visible tip of the iceberg. The far greater cost was an unseen one. Indiscriminate downsizing, brought on by poorly thought-through re-engineering activity, practically decimated employee morale. It is common knowledge today that downsizing doesn't just affect those who leave, but also those who stay, a phenomenon recognized in psychology as the 'survivor syndrome'. Seeing no clear rationale for superficial reorganizations, those who stay go through a unique cocktail of emotions—guilt for having survived the mayhem, mistrust of management and their varying strategy, stress through the extra workload they now had and the fear of being the next in a seemingly random lottery.

The chart (fig. 2.1) drawn from Gallup Inc.'s substantive database on employee engagement amply demonstrates how the employee engagement profile of US organizations flips during phases of downsizing.

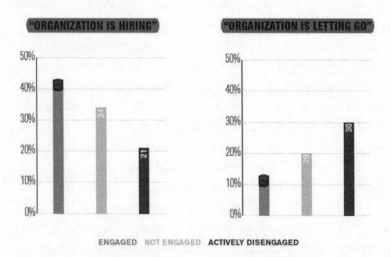

Source: Gallup Inc. (State of the American Workplace)
Fig 2.1: The Impact of Restructuring on Employee Engagement

Gallup defines engaged employees as those who 'are psychologically committed to their jobs and likely to be making positive contributions to their organizations'.[22]

In my opinion, when the case for reorganization isn't appreciable and well accepted, the psychological cost paid by the continuing many could easily dwarf the economic costs saved through the departing few.

THE DEMOLITION OF LOYALTY

On the one hand, the transfer of financial and employment risk from the organization to its talent has resulted in an age of transactional employment, where an employee's loyalty is transient in nature. With hopping from job-to-job as a career strategy becoming more socially accepted, recruitment site Careerbuilder. com reports that 'by the age of 35, 25 per cent of workers have held five jobs or more. For workers aged 55 and older, 20 per cent have held ten jobs or more'.[23]

The portability of long-term benefits has resulted in historically low disincentives for hopping jobs. A 2016 survey by professional networking site LinkedIn found that 90 per cent of all professionals on their network are interested in hearing about job opportunities, while 36 per cent are actively browsing for job openings. And this is an accelerating trend. In 2014, this number was 25 per cent.[24]

On the other hand, it isn't just employees who are less loyal. As Wharton management professor Adam Cobb explains, 'My loyalty to the firm is contingent on my firm's loyalty to me. But there is one party in that exchange which has tremendously more power, and that is the firm.'[25] The spike in restructuring activity since 1990 suggests there has been an erosion of loyalty on both ends of the employment contract.

LABOUR INTENSIVE IN THE KNOWLEDGE AGE

We now recognize that after a century or so of relative job security, the concept of stable long-term employment as the default career option is fast fading into history. In fast-paced business environments which put a premium on speed and flexibility, both the tone and tenor of the legacy employment contract makes it unwieldy and resistant to change.

The factors driving this change are already in motion. The shift of financial risk from employer to employee was the first elemental shift. Absolute portability of long-term benefits was the second. Restructuring as management strategy was the third. The fourth, as we see in the chapter immediately following this one, is the rise of knowledge work and how it has effectively detached the value of labour from the time and space in which it is performed. In later chapters, we will see how emerging trends like machine learning and artificial intelligence are forcing human endeavour away from simple, algorithmic and repetitive tasks towards solving problems and incubating new ideas. It is the human mind, as opposed to the human body, which has been an underutilized resource for far too long.

It is important to remind ourselves that all these changes are largely consequential in nature, including the decline in loyalty. They have all partly come about due to the larger global shift from localized labour-intensive economies to a larger and better networked global knowledge economy.

Organizations that succeed in this knowledge economy aren't going to be pure-play insourced, neither will they be totally outsourced in nature. That would be too extreme a social experiment in this day and age, and hence unsustainable in the near future.

As we saw in chapter one, every organization has a distinct talent recipe, defined as a perfect blend of internal and external capability customized to fit the needs of a specific business. We will still have a fair number of employees on long-term contracts. But organizations must get much better at discerning the roles they want to see these employees play and the way they manage them.

The mechanics that go into finding and transitioning a new full-time employee in an era of high volatility, disruption and low loyalty strongly suggest that full-time employment in the knowledge age will continue to shrink and the acquisition of external capability will continue to grow till organizations achieve their ideal talent recipe. The smartest talent doesn't fear this arrangement, and neither do the innovative organizations which employ them.

So why do we continue to see organizations rely on headcount to grow? A part of the answer is simply management inertia. Many managers still prefer to 'own' positions on an organization chart. However, this is a minor reason. The major one, quite simply, is that there is no credible alternative. Contingent talent just hasn't been voluminous enough or of the right quality to truly compete with those seeking full-time jobs. But the human cloud is about to change that.

Like the first factor—the transfer of financial risk—described earlier started unpacking employment in the late 1970s, history may acknowledge that in late 2009, the growing trend of contingent work first condensed into a discernible human cloud. Because that was the year when the global economy stabilized after the financial crisis which directly displaced over 20 million workers, and affected the careers of over 100 million more across the world. Further, 2009 was also the year when web 2.0, 3G telephony and cloud computing matured, as evinced by the rise of digital infrastructure and smart devices.

These shifts have, in turn, fast-tracked a global ecosystem for smart capability. Over the subsequent chapters, we will deconstruct this global system as it currently stands and what it may look like in 2030 and beyond.

3

THE FUTURE-READY ORGANIZATION

Come forth into the light of things, let Nature be your teacher.
—William Wordsworth

A NEW DEFINITION

We began this book with a new definition for 'talent' in the new age. Rather than define talent as a small pool of internal resources—such as a few high potentials, a limited list of senior successors or an in-demand demographic cluster—this book looks at talent in its broadest sense. In Future-Ready Organizations, talent is 'any capability which creates economic value'.

Most business owners I discuss this with tend to agree with the new definition. In practice, they are less concerned with owning vast masses of headcount, being interested instead in having access to the best skills at the right place and at the right time. It makes economic sense too because it allows for the deconstruction of work itself—from a nebulous superset of activities which consumes a 9-to-5 workday into a set of value-creating actions or projects.

The fact that this is already happening is also undeniable. We see evidence of this in shrinking headcounts, increased outsourcing, an explosion of contingent talent, the emergence of global networks, spikes in M&A activity or the rise of acquisitions as the new R&D strategy. And we see them in more 'built for purpose' institutional partnerships.

Much of this has been driven by immediate or tactical needs such as cost or regulatory pressures, the demand for rapid international expansion, a desire to catch up with new competition or to copy industry best practices and hence, without an overarching design or perhaps even strategic intent.

The good news is that when seen from a macro vantage-point, almost all organizations participate in the distributed talent economy in some shape or form today. The competitive and cost realities of 21st-century business have forced us all off the ground and onto the first step of the distributed and dynamic capability ladder. We are all on different rungs, though. Some businesses are on higher rungs, and racing still ahead, while others are barely on the first or second one and still feeling a little overwhelmed at having left terra firma.

THREE TRENDS REDRAWING THE FUNDAMENTAL ARCHITECTURE OF WORK

As the knowledge and digital economies accelerate, almost all changes to the world of work can be traced back to three primary causal trends.

The first trend, as we saw in the previous chapter, is the erosion of loyalty on both ends of the employment equation.

The second, which has come in more recently, deals with the rapid rise of high-quality contingent and automated capability. A company's source-pool now includes millions of distinctively skilled people, willing to work part-time, short-term and on specific tasks rather than full-time jobs. Further, as we will see in chapters that follow, intelligent machines are at the cusp of taking large chunks of simple, repetitive and algorithmic tasks away from human workforces. Taken together, the human cloud, surrounded by a much larger and infinitely more disruptive mechanical cloud, will profoundly change the cost-benefit and location-time dynamics of distributed capability.

The final trend deals with the global nature of work. Not only does the modern business now have access to millions of highly skilled people, they could be located anywhere in the world. In practical terms, what this means is that in a digitally enabled world, all businesses are global.

These three trends are complementary yet connected. They also show us how—for the first time since the assembly line—the fundamental architecture of business is changing. As a direct consequence, savvy business leaders are starting to intuitively recognize that to be successful in the digital age, an organization's structure and architecture need to move well beyond the narrow confines of the (industrial-era) pyramid. And this topic already sits at the top of the boardroom agenda. How do we know this?

Sometime in April 2017, consulting firm Mercer released its 2017 Global Talent Trends report[26] which showed that a whopping 93 per cent of responding organizations were planning a fundamental organization redesign over the next two years. This was, by far, the most pressing priority in Mercer's opinion.

A couple of months earlier, in February 2017, rival consulting major Deloitte had issued its independently sourced 2017 Global Human Capital Trends Survey[27] which had found that 88 per cent of all the executives in their sample rated 'building the organization of the future' as the most important challenge they faced. According to Deloitte, this was a universal trend. A total of 96 per cent of executives in India prioritized this issue, as did 89 per cent in China, 88 per cent in UK and 87 per cent in US (fig. 3.1).

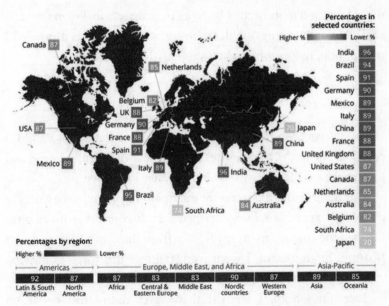

Source: Rewriting the Rules for the Digital Age', 2017 Deloitte Global
Human Capital Trends, Deloitte University Press

Fig. 3.1: Organization of the Future: Global Response

Similar to the Mercer study which was to follow, the executives
Deloitte surveyed also rated this as the number one challenge they
were facing.

These reports aren't isolated. Several think-tanks and surveys
reveal a strong dissonance with inflexible industrial-era organization
design—structures which trap the majority of an organization's
talent in fixed job descriptions and rigid leadership hierarchies.
These constructs no longer serve the needs of modern business.

So why aren't we changing these structures right away?
Deloitte's research included a telling statistic. Of the 88 per cent
who prioritized 'building organizations of the future' as a need,
'only 11 per cent of survey respondents believe they understand
how to build an organization of the future'.

This book, hence, comes perfectly timed for an audience in search
of deeper understanding. It provides an expansive canvas, along with

the colours and tools needed by modern managers to design the ideal capability architecture for their business. And there is a powerful metaphor in nature which shows us exactly how to do so.

UNIVERSAL ENERGY

I have always been fascinated by the nature of waves. As a child, I could sit for hours on the ocean-front near our family home and look at the sea. The waves made the water look alive.

But wading into the water for the first time proved to be a deeply dissonant experience. I was terrified. My discomfort reduced once I gained the courage to lift my feet up from the ocean floor and start floating. In an instant, I went from fighting this force to flowing with it—from resisting it to dancing with it.

Later in school, I learned that waves didn't just occur on the surface of the ocean. They were all around us. Indeed, electromagnetic energy—one of the fundamental building blocks of the universe—exists in waves of varying frequencies. Some, like radio waves, could be a hundred metres wide, while others, like highly toxic gamma rays, are smaller than an atom. Together, these waves dominate the physical realm unlike any other form of matter known to humans.

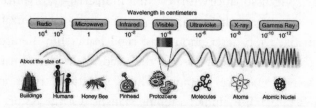

Source: NASA[28]

Fig. 3.2: The Electromagnetic Spectrum

In fig. 3.2, visible light or white light occupies a tiny fraction of the full spectrum—a narrow band between 700 nanometres and 400 nanometres. Yet, because the human eye has evolved to see just white light, it has dominated our consciousness since the dawn of civilization.

By contrast, our awareness of other energy waves is much more recent. Around 150 years old to be exact. It took Michael Faraday, Heinrich Rudolf Hertz and James Clerk Maxwell's experiments in the middle of the 19th century to reveal the existence of high and low-frequency energy waves.

But such is the power of human ingenuity that once the spectrum was mapped by the late 19th century, we found practical applications for recently discovered electromagnetic radiation within a few years. For example, Wilhelm Conrad Roentgen discovered X-rays in 1895, and within five short years, rudimentary X-ray machines were being used by doctors to fix bones. Similarly, the German physicist Heinrich Hertz discovered radio waves in the 1890s while experimenting with the theories of J.C. Maxwell. By 1906, the first AM radio network was already broadcasting music and by the early 1950s, astronomers had already used radio waves to map the entire Milky Way. By 1931, the tiny microwave, also discovered by Hertz, was running wireless communications across the English Channel, before powering radar machines in World War II and making popcorn on kitchen counters just a few years later.

Astonishingly, all of this happened within a hundred years of humankind proving that waves didn't just occur on the surface of the sea.

FULL SPECTRUM THINKING

My research shows that the electromagnetic spectrum is a commanding metaphor for organizational capability. Just as the human eye has evolved to see nothing but white light, organizations have traditionally focused on just a small subset of their capability—internal headcount, or the visible few.

However, when you look at the entire spectrum of capability available to an organization, you suddenly open endless talent frequencies to access human energy—in real time and at significant cost efficiencies.

A vibrant capability spectrum already exists before us. Besides, it isn't just the technology firms and the sharing economy which thrive on distributed or dynamic capabilities. Since the early 1990s, the rapid rise of strategic outsourcing, freelancing, service supply chains, globalization and digital connectivity have ensured that most organizations already use a varied mix of capabilities. Yet, most do so in a largely intuitive and disconnected manner, without thinking about talent governance or strategy.

The main culprit here, without question, is the industrial-era design of narrow functional silos. This has meant that the HR department largely ignores anything beyond internal capability. It continues to interpret its purpose through the headcount lens. All this, while the finance function drives acquisitions or outsourcing using a distinctly cost-driven agenda and the procurement team brings in vendors on a strict diet of narrowly defined service level agreements. For their part, business leaders may directly manage contractors, consultants, business affiliations or joint ventures with little functional support.

Hence, in practice, our scattered capability arrangements are a product of a largely tactical and disconnected system. Imagine how powerful they could be with a little synchronicity and design thinking thrown in!

THE DYNAMIC CAPABILITY SPECTRUM

The universe has a natural rhythm which enables harmony and synchronicity and there is wisdom in recognizing that effort and contribution—as forms of organizational energy—may operate similarly too. Taking the metaphor forward, imagine the size of waves in the electromagnetic spectrum representing the relational dynamics of modern business.

If so, then large radio wavelengths would reflect an organization's strategic alliances and significant long-term associations. Medium frequencies would represent significant and critical individuals—be they internal and external talent—who anchor day-to-day activities within a business. The densely packed, almost microscopic waves, on the other extreme, could signify high-frequency or algorithmic 'micro-tasks' potentially managed by crowdsourced arrangements.

If we imagine this as a continuous and synchronous system, representing nine sources of human capability, it would probably look something like fig. 3.3.

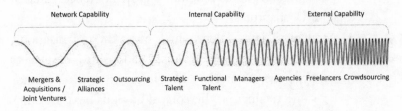

Fig. 3.3: Nine Sources of Human Capability

During the research phase of this book, I found that many leaders intuitively recognize all nine wavelengths in the illustration. The nine reflect common capability choices available to modern business. What the illustration also shows is that in the world of digitally enabled business, most organizations draw capability from three distinct sources:

1. *Network Capability*: The big wavelengths represent our significant big-ticket associations and institutional arrangements. In most cases, these arrangements are multi-year and provide rapid access to complementary capability, entry into new markets or a distribution of risk. In a post-globalized world, these arrangements have proven useful to

both growth and efficiency. Consider the two trillion dollars worth of outsourced manufacturing and services that these arrangements have driven or the exponential rise in mergers and acquisitions. The catalogue of institutional capability on offer also includes joint ventures, network collaborations, brand alliances and other vendor arrangements beyond outsourcing such as the increasingly popular Software as a Service (SaaS).

2. *Internal Capability*: Denotes owned talent, but in a much more focused manner than in the past. As this talent tends to be the most expensive and the least flexible by nature, it must be reserved for roles with a direct impact on either revenue, organizational renewal or growth. Hence, internal capability constitutes:

   ♦ Strategic Talent: Talent which owns the organization's most critical revenue streams, relationships, customers or products. Strategic talent is either a value creator or value retainer, at the core of any business. In other words, strategic talent is also your Balance-Sheet Talent, and must be viewed, managed and cultivated as a long-term asset.

   This definition is a critical one, because the century-old accounting standards have always defined assets as 'resources with economic value' owned by an organization; yet the standards have not evolved beyond land and machinery, in line with the evolution of business. In the knowledge era, it is often the inherent contribution of key people in key roles which keeps the business growing. It is this group that we call strategic talent.

   ♦ Functional Talent: This is a small group of deep domain-experts who design and govern functional or deep technical agenda within the organization. It is important to note that they are not executors. As much of functional delivery can now be done through software applications or external vendors, we don't need armies of executors anymore. Hence, the internal talent we own must be calibrated to drive the technical and functional innovation agenda within the business. In this book, we will refer to this group as *Functional Innovators*.

♦ Management Talent: Industrial-era people managers were essentially tasked with supervising and driving performance within a finite set of internal resources. In the future, management's key inputs will be the organization of dynamic capability spectrum. Finding the right people, at the right time and at the right price to create economic value for an organization, and also getting the whole spectrum of distributed resources to work harmoniously.

Learning from the success of Agile systems, management talent must possess deep project management skills and the ability to work with complex processes and technology. This makes managers themselves more mobile and to an extent, interchangeable or fungible within a company's talent system.

The mobility of managers is critical. By imagining management as a fluid resource with catalytic properties, our aim should be to build a community of professionals who can be deployed wherever needed most. Enhancing mobility also helps us steer clear of the most crippling developments of pyramidical structures—the creation of fiefdoms, where managers stockpile resources and resist changes to the status quo.

It is fungibility that makes management one of the most powerful ingredients within a distributed talent system. Like emulsifiers, they integrate the efforts of all other ingredients. In Future-Ready Organizations, a mobile and fungible management team fulfils two specific outcomes—it cultivates capability and curates contribution within a dynamic talent system.

3. *External Capability*: This represents what research suggests is the fastest growing part of human capability spectrum—contingent talent.

The contingent skills we can access today exist in a spectrum range. At one end of this range we have professional or agency talent with niche expertise, which could be priced at thousands of dollars an hour. Think of the highly specialized international arbitration lawyer who may only be needed on a case-by-case basis. In the middle of the range exists a vibrant and digitally-enabled freelance marketplace populated by millions of project hires with more commoditized skills. Contracted only when needed, on near-term assignments, these project-based professionals are freely available on short-term hire and are frequently compensated at reasonable hourly-wage levels. Consider application designers or web professionals as examples in the middle of this contingent band. At the other end of this assortment of contingent skills exists the micro-tasker—a group of micro-entrepreneurs and crowdsources which are fuelling the sharing economy and disrupting industries as diverse as transportation (Uber), hospitality (Airbnb), content creation (Amazon Mechanical Turk), all the way to logistics (Deliveroo). It is important to note that definition of a micro-task is any body of work which can be contracted, completed and paid for in four hours or less.

When considering the power of external talent and the contingent workforce, it serves us well to remember the purpose of dynamic capability systems we reviewed in chapter one. Remember, some of the smartest people who can create value for your business will never carry your employee ID. Yet, your capability management strategy must aim to get them to the table at the right time, at the right place and at the right price.

When we put all three sources of capability (internal, external and network) together, fig. 3.4 is what the spectrum of dynamic capability available to you today looks like.

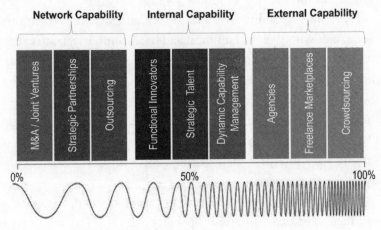

Fig. 3.4: Spectrum of Dynamic Capability

THE ARCHITECTURE OF MODERN BUSINESS

Every business exists within a specific talent context and is engineered from a distinct mix of capabilities. No two competitors use the same capability mix, even though they compete for a share of the same customer's wallet. This makes getting the talent recipe of a business right, and turn it into a significant operational (and competitive) advantage.

A broad and dynamic capability strategy helps us achieve this. It gives us the ability to map and think through both our current and future talent architecture. By bringing together perspectives from functions like finance, HR, procurement, legal and IT, among others, it allows a business leader to stitch an expansive capability tapestry which best fits her or his business. Once this is done, we can begin to further enhance access, governance and value from a distributed and blended talent system. Further, by compiling disparate sources of human capability into a single frame, the model also gives us the ability to analyze how competitors within a single industry use capability in vastly different ways and equally, how digitization affects an industry's capability mix.

Dynamic capability models also highlight why traditional companies with their pyramidical and headcount driven structures are struggling to compete with disruptive newcomers who are digital in both orientation and structure. For example, during the research phase of this book, when we were still investigating the nine pillars of human capability which now constitute the Dynamic Capability Spectrum, we helped several organizations of varying sizes interpret their organization's capability architecture using this framework.

In practice, we found several instances of competitors who had made distinctly different capability choices. Here is one such example of three vastly different capability structures operating within a single industry:

DYNAMIC CAPABILITY CASE STUDY #1:
THE TRADITIONAL INDUSTRY LEADER

The organization in the first example is a market share leader with an eighty-year history of impressive returns to shareholders. Having suffered during the 2008-09 financial crisis which had forced job cuts, the company was now back to hiring large numbers of employees in line with customer growth projections. Fig. 3.5 is what their current capability architecture looked like, in terms of people deployed.

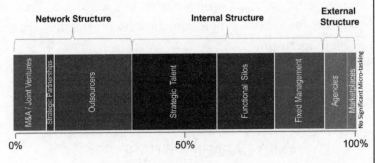

Fig. 3.5: Current Capability Architecture:
Traditional Industry Leader

This kind of structure is very common today. Because it reflects the industrial DNA that most traditional companies grew up with—largely internal, coupled with the relatively recent cost-driven push to outsource transactional and non-core work to vendors.

The capability frequencies in the figure show us an organization with lots of overhead, stockpiled functional expertise and multilayer management hierarchies.

Also, while outsourcing is often a good strategy to combat bloat, in this case I would hazard that outsourcing is reserved for transactional or marginal capabilities because it doesn't seem to have driven dramatic internal efficiency.

Traditional capability systems often look like this because of legacy culture and operating mindsets. Leaders think in terms of headcount, not capability. Entrenched functional boundaries as well as outdated job descriptions aren't renegotiated in line with technology shifts. As a direct consequence, this structure drives linear and incremental performance along past trajectories. In disruptive times and phases of industry evolution, this capability structure can struggle to compete with more nimble, flexible and cost-efficient competitors. And we have profiled one such competitor to the traditional business you see above. Let's see how this new-age competitor structures itself using the dynamic capability spectrum.

The company profiled in the next case study was in direct competition with the one earlier and had been chasing them steadily in the race for market share.

DYNAMIC CAPABILITY CASE STUDY #2:
THE DIGITAL-AGE COMPETITOR

A much younger company, which was started fifteen years ago and still run by one of the co-founders, was fast gaining a reputation for customer responsiveness, innovative products and for attracting younger customers through its strong digital service delivery platform. Their capability architecture looked different too, and when their executives explained why, it made perfect sense (fig. 3.6).

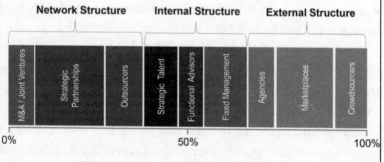

Fig. 3.6: Current Capability Architecture:
The Digital-Age Competitor

Founded just after the turn of the millennium by a group of friends who had all quit well-settled jobs for a shot at an entrepreneurial life, what immediately struck me was how its founders had recognized the internet and software as core tools of the trade.

Consequently, the leadership team had eschewed investments in brick and mortar distribution in favour of strategic partnerships with established retailers or straight to internet solutions. Collaborations and brand alliances were in their DNA. In addition, they employed a flexible contracted workforce, which worked closely with internal resources on project delivery. Contract work was also positioned as a hiring path for permanent roles.

What was impressively different about this management team as compared to the previous company was that its leaders saw themselves primarily as a technology team trying to recast the industry through innovate approaches and products. Yet they constantly worried about 'not being tech enough'. One of these leaders pointed me towards another company, a fledgling start-up with impressive venture backing that was looking to become the voice of the industry's customers.

DYNAMIC CAPABILITY CASE STUDY #3:
THE DISRUPTIVE NEW ENTRANT

Founded by two young MBA graduates in their mid-thirties, this third company was a digital aggregator of products. Built solely around the customer's need for greater information and choice, they didn't see themselves competing with the industry heavyweights. On the contrary, they saw all industry players as potential collaborators, and their architecture reflected this collaborative DNA in more ways than one (fig. 3.7).

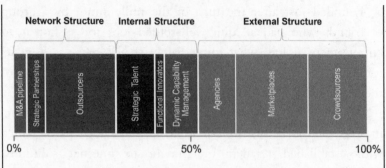

Fig. 3.7: Current Capability Architecture: Collaborative Company

Their capability frequencies revealed some interesting choices. Firstly, their internal structure was the smallest, in terms of people deployed. This, in itself, isn't unique. Most successful young businesses throughout history have been incubated by small groups of employees. The spectrum of choice available to a young firm today allows them the historically unique prospect of growth without owning every capability needed to fuel that growth. This is a noteworthy advantage of dynamic capability systems. It isn't without reason that many start-ups today often end up punching significantly above their weight. They see key talent as their greatest asset and build entire organizations around this 'balance-sheet' capability.

This is exactly what I found with this disruptive newcomer. Almost all internal roles were focused on high-value outcomes, whereas transient technology skills, most commoditized work and even functional support roles were all contracted out or insourced through vendor arrangements. When I asked them to define strategic talent, the founders described it as 'roles dedicated to either proprietary technology, business development or product innovation'.

Another aspect of their capability model which stood out was the use of a fluid external workforce to supplement and support project completion. Almost all media, content, graphics, advertising and even HR tasks like hiring were resourced through on-demand arrangements or retained agencies.

YOUR COMPETITION DOESN'T LOOK LIKE YOU ANYMORE

What we see happening across these three examples is being replicated in numerous industries even as you read these words. Established industry leaders continue carrying industrial-era values into the digital age, chief among them being the relative inability to think far beyond the ubiquity of full-time employment.

This is an existential challenge because lining up opposite them are an army of digital natives and disruptive innovators, capable of achieving exponential scale and speed through a radically new recipe of owned, borrowed and collaborative capability. The outcome is an explosion of disruptive customer propositions, which can be fulfilled at a fraction of the industry's average transaction cost. Even if we look at just the three examples discussed, the diagram (fig. 3.8) shows what competition within a singular industry can look like today.

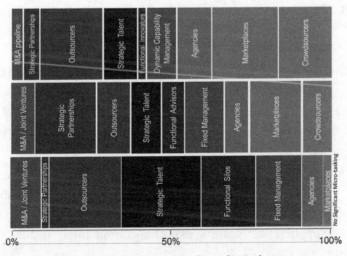

Fig. 3.8: Competition in a Singular Industry

POWERED BY A BLENDED WORKFORCE

In a nutshell, Dynamic Capability Management is a new way of looking at business design, structure, talent and skills. It helps modern business cope better with volatility, rapid growth and financial risk—both an asset and expense risk—in a much smarter manner. Some of the most successful tech companies and industry disruptors today are true masters at this. And it isn't just the disruptors who have excelled at this. Traditional players have used dynamic capability models to fundamentally transform their business. One of the most dramatic examples is how Steve Jobs turned around Apple Computers on his return as CEO in 1997. When seen in hindsight, it was the smart capability choices Jobs made which had a material impact on Apple's rise from near bankruptcy to becoming the richest company in the world in a short span of twenty years. These choices allowed Apple to rise at unprecedented speeds for a large business, translating each breakthrough idea into unprecedented scale and growth. Here is how Jobs built the new Apple:

1. He ensured research and development, product design and operating system development were all done in-house, deploying his best balance-sheet talent in key roles.
2. As Apple scaled its device business through the pathbreaking iPod and iPhone lines, Jobs made a conscious choice—in the face of stiff criticism—to outsource the assembly of the devices, mainly to Foxconn and later to Pegatron in China and Taiwan.
3. While no one knows the exact list of suppliers which Apple uses for all its component needs, its devices are assembled from a host of individual parts sourced from over fifty key suppliers. Companies like Qualcomm, Intel, Toshiba and

Texas Instruments often figure high on this list. Interestingly, few know that Apple's most significant competitor in the smartphone market, Samsung, is also a major iPhone component supplier, making the OLED screen and DRAM chips used on successive generations of iPhones.

4. Another key choice that allowed Apple to reach customers in all parts of the world at scale was the choice to set up its 'reseller' network. By plugging in tens of thousands of independent entrepreneurs into its distribution strategy, it could avoid spending huge amounts of resources and time on brick-and-mortar stores. Similarly, after-sales service for Apple's products were also done through a tightly controlled network of partners spanning the globe, keeping devices running with high-quality repairs, all the while providing customers an extension of the Apple experience.

5. And finally, the true masterstroke was Job's decision in 2008 to open up the development of applications which would run on the new iPhone to thousands of developers through the App Store. Doing so, he created the first true digital platform connecting millions of customers with an initial community of a few hundred app developers. This kept Apple's internal resources lean, yet allowed over two million apps to flourish via a competitive and regulated marketplace. To me, this was the first truly crowdsourced technology model and its success can be seen through the meteoric success of billion-dollar app development companies like Rovio (famous for the Angry Birds game), all the while making Apple's core product, its smartphone, into one of the most successful products in history.

It would be an understatement to say that Steve Jobs was a business leader well ahead of his time. Yet he wasn't the only one experimenting with dynamic capability. Gaming company Sony was too, as was Microsoft and tens of others. However, Steve Jobs was the first leader to transform his entire company using dynamic capability thinking.

The trend has clearly caught on. Even the most traditional tech companies like Cisco are using what they call 'dynamic teams'. P&G uses its 'connect and develop' platform to connect a thousand internal R&D employees to 1.5 million scientists and chemists who could assist new product development. Almost all businesses are evolving into flexible collaboratives. Cooperatives, like milk distributor Amul in India, have been doing this for years, but today, real-time data and collaboration/platform technology is transforming the maturity with which we manage distributed talent.

THE NEED FOR DYNAMIC LEADERSHIP

Often, business leaders, who have spent a career growing through the ranks of a pyramidical organization, struggle to imagine how the business could look different. The real-life incident in the next case study highlights exactly why.

DYNAMIC CAPABILITY CASE STUDY #4: THE LEADERSHIP BREAKTHROUGH

A few months ago, we were leading a cross-functional capability review at the European headquarters of a Fortune 500 company. The goal of this four-week project was to analyze and present a full spectrum view of a key manufacturing division. I had worked with this client before but was meeting with the divisional leadership team for the first time, at a project kickoff meeting of sorts. The Managing Director of the division, sitting directly opposite me at the other end of an unusually long boardroom table, was uncharacteristically silent as I began to explain the framework and project to follow.

We were anticipating this. The pre-meeting brief had described him as extremely action-oriented, with little time for abstract concepts. A career engineer who had grown through the ranks building customized industrial machines, each worth millions of dollars, for demanding clients, he had as industrial-era a DNA as humanly possible.

Around twenty minutes into the meeting, as we were dissecting the capability architecture of another manufacturing company, purely as an example to explain the new spectrum of choices now available, I think the penny suddenly dropped.

'Hold on a moment, Gyan,' he interrupted. 'Our big customers have been telling us that we are around 30 per cent more expensive than some of our competitors, and we haven't won a price-sensitive bid in years.'

'Go on,' I said.

'But we are a clear quality leader, with a design edge. As a result, we have consciously chased high-end business and landed several high-profile contracts.' He was clearly thinking aloud here. 'But I never really understood what a lot of the customers who couldn't afford us have been telling me for years—they wanted access to our design and engineering capabilities, even if they couldn't manufacture with us,' he said, looking right at me. 'I think this framework now gives us the tools to do so. These customers want to work with us. Our brand means something to them.'

He turned to his operations chief with a decisive vigour in his voice. 'We must build a division which drives deep partnerships with the best manufacturing facilities around the world and gives these customers access to our best design experts. We could still underwrite and manage the project.'

And with that, the thirty-year manufacturing veteran had the beginnings of a roadmap to reinvent his business. He eventually sponsored a team to scope a more detailed business proposition and propose what the capability architecture of this business could look like. A couple of months later, the executive team finally signed off (fig. 3.9).

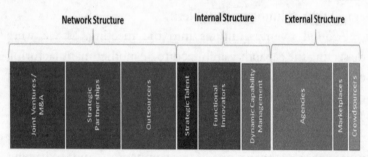

Fig. 3.9: Capability Architecture: Manufacturing Designs Division

A decades-old and highly respected manufacturing leader on the cusp of disruption is now in the process of inventing a future-ready design business, which could drive industry-wide collaborations. A scenario scarcely imaginable weeks before our meeting.

Like a telescope helps make greater sense of the night sky, at its core the Dynamic Capability Spectrum is a lens to help business leaders review both current capability choices and future opportunities available to them.

And it isn't just the CEO in this case who struggles to let go of leadership values anchored in the industrial-age. Leaders at all levels do. And the prognosis for this changing naturally isn't good.

Many leadership development strategies fall short because they confuse leader development with leadership development. An easy mistake to make in the short term, yet perniciously lethal in the long term. Leader development is about ensuring a pipeline of leaders with the right skills for the roles they perform. Leadership development, on the other hand, is about the evolution of an organization's leadership culture.

Investments in leader development result in a skill and knowledge-based culture, while a focus on leadership development results in a future-ready purpose-based culture. In the same vein, while the short-term agenda deals with performance and profitability, I would also argue that an organization's long-term agenda must prioritize innovations which enhance the organization's positive contributions to society and all its stakeholders. From a dynamic capability perspective, a future-ready leadership culture is best exemplified not just through the engagement of internal talent, but equally by how leaders perceive, empower, integrate, reward and support their distributed talent.

WHERE DO YOU SPEND YOUR CAPABILITY DOLLARS?

Coming back to the subject of dynamic capability strategy, the final view we need to create is about our current cost of capability.

In all the examples presented thus far, we have mapped individuals or communities of people who inhabit our talent ecosystem—our fixed, flexible and networked headcount. Another powerful way to look at our talent ecosystem is through the cost lens. Where do we spend our capability dollars? This can be an eye-opener too, as often the cost of capability—both owned and contracted—dominates the expense side of an organization's profit-and-loss statement.

That's exactly what one company found when it used the Dynamic Capability Spectrum to anchor a debate on overall internal and external talent spends.

DYNAMIC CAPABILITY CASE STUDY #5:
THE COST LENS

At a fast-paced technology company, with significant scope for future growth, the executive team was surprised to see how explosive, yet haphazard, growth had led to shocking bloat in one particular dynamic capability pillar—outsourcing. The analysis showed that outsourcing contracts signed by different divisions in the company totalled over one in three dollars spent on aggregate capability (fig 3.10).

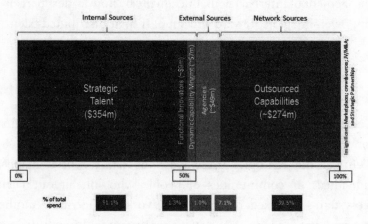

Fig. 3.10: Dynamic Capability Costs

While it was comforting that of the $700 million annual capability spend, almost half was being spent on strategic (in this case defined as revenue, product and governance critical) talent, both high outsourcing costs and the low fungibility of managers emerged as a direct concern. Barely 1 per cent of their capability system was truly mobile and ready to redeploy at short notice.

As we can see in all the five case studies, dynamic capability is a key enabler of organizational renewal. It can create unprecedented insight into an existing talent ecosystem and anchor critical executive debate on future capability choices.

Every business exists within a specific talent context and possesses a distinct talent recipe which meets the specific needs of its customers and other stakeholders.

Before we establish this recipe, it is imperative we understand all the nine pillars of dynamic capability available to you, as well as track the emergence of a tenth and possibly eleventh source capability on the horizon. This is exactly what the essence of this book, from this point on, helps us do.

4

SOURCES OF DYNAMIC CAPABILITY
Your Internal Talent

Better a diamond with a flaw than a pebble without.
—Confucius

The previous chapter explained that every competitive business already has a full-spectrum talent recipe. Your organization has one too. And I am sure you are curious to figure out what it looks like. This is a great place to be at this stage of the book because curiosity is a great ally. It helps us ask new questions and motivates us to travel beyond the familiar.

Before we style an organization-wide talent recipe, it is wise to acquire a deeper understanding of the nine types of human capability a modern organization has access to (fig. 4.1).

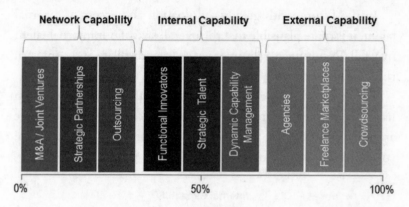

Fig. 4.1: Types of Human Capability Accessible to Organizations

And the best place to start is from the very heart of the framework—internal talent, which anchors the full spectrum of the enterprise.

FROM CONCRETE PYRAMIDS TO SCAFFOLDED ORGANIZATIONS

As internal talent is the least flexible and most expensive part of your capability recipe, one of the key tests of any internal structure is the ability to survive economic volatility and downturns without the need for large-scale structural changes. This normally denotes one of two possible things:

1. These roles aren't short term or transactional. They contribute as much to long-term success as they do to short-term results.
2. The roles are instrumental to the efficiency of the overall business.

In the future, with greater automation and access to external talent, it is quite plausible that the overall size of our internal talent may fall. Resulting in a slimmer yet sharper distillate of the internal roles we have today.

However, unlike the past, where fair-weather job rationalization has delivered negative returns (as we saw in chapter two), this time around we must aim to transform not just the shape of our internal structures but its purpose too (fig. 4.2).

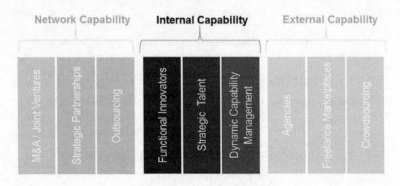

Fig. 4.2: Internal Structure

As the foundations of future business will be more digital than physical, it is critical that our internal structure represents new and growing competencies rather than a cosmetic restructuring of old ones. A great way to achieve this is to consciously see future organizations as anything but a pyramid.

The industrial-era pyramid and the organization charts they represent aren't all bad. They continue to deliver powerful outcomes, such as clear accountabilities, linear communication flows, equitable distribution of effort, visible career paths and competence development frameworks and so on. This is the good part.

But equally, their rigid construction has stood in the way of adaptability, collaboration and renewal. We see evidence of this in wasteful layers of hierarchy, entrenched and self-serving fiefdoms, destructive politics and pointless internal competition. Built for a different age, their inherent inflexibility makes it near impossible to redeploy capability or move with the markets, without the use of surgical force.

Rather than an internal structure built around concrete hierarchies and inflexible competencies, the nimble and digitally enabled organizations of the future must be built for speed, flexibility and collaboration. This doesn't necessarily mean the pyramid must be abandoned in favour of another shape. Any fixed structure will ossify over time, leading to many of the same ills we see today.

I prefer to use what social leadership guru Julian Stodd describes as 'Social Scaffolding',[29] which signifies an interactive structure which consciously creates common space and time for social learning and co-creation.

According to Stodd, by de-emphasizing the formal structure, we allow a powerful yet flexible social structure to grow in its place. The freedom this affords allows employees to collaborate on ideas which matter to the organization as a whole.

What this means in practice is that:

1. Internal roles must be reserved for high impact tasks, which add direct and unambiguous economic value to organizational goals.
2. Internal talent must be organized with the freedom to reach across boundaries to learn, ideate and collaborate.

To get closer to understanding how successful new-age businesses and industry disruptors are using internal roles, let's dive deeper into the three sources of internal capability within the Future-Ready Organization.

STRATEGIC TALENT

Strategic Talent is the group of people that form the very fulcrum of value within a business, and it is important to recognize from the very beginning that in this case, 'strategic' does not mean 'senior-most'. In fact, very few senior managers may qualify. Instead, this term represents all the value creators and value retainers within a business.

Value creators are hunters and innovators. The hunters drive sales or acquire new long-term customer accounts, and innovators denominate your new product design or are your key R&D experts. Without value creators, your sales growth, product innovation and intellectual property growth, all just stall.

The value retainers sit alongside the value creators. They are the farmers every business needs. The value retainers deliver the health of legacy revenue streams, existing client relationships and the delivery of current products. They are the drivers of your current profit-and-loss statement. If you sell online, it includes those that manage this channel. If your sales are face-to-face, this includes your sales and marketing teams that help deliver the current quarter's numbers. It also includes those delivering current products to existing customers. It is the value retainers who anchor your entire organic customer delivery system.

BALANCE-SHEET TALENT

Together, value-creating and value-retaining roles ensure both stability and profitability for the long term. Which is why I call them your 'Balance-Sheet Talent'.

Balance-Sheet Talent, by definition, must be resilient enough to largely survive both industry boom and bust cycles. Hence, it is important to treat them like a revenue-critical fixed asset involved in one of three outcomes:

1. Revenue producing relationships
2. Core product development
3. Long-term intellectual property

Any roles that don't strictly serve these outcomes could theoretically be redesigned to fit into one of the other eight sources of the Dynamic Capability Spectrum.

This clarity is important because almost everyone in an organization would like to be called strategic, making this capability bucket very susceptible to bloat. One way to avoid this is by building a customized view of what it means to be strategic. Fig. 4.3 represents how one organization defined their strategic talent and ended up with eight specific outcomes which ring-fenced a few thousand roles.

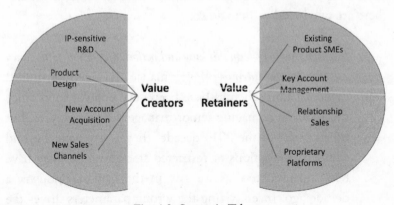

Fig. 4.3: Strategic Talent

It took a few weeks and a fair amount of debate to get the right roles mapped within this box, but it was a necessary pre-requisite for what had to follow next–a reaffirmation of commitment.

REBUILDING TRUST

Balance-sheet talent must have a long career horizon with the organization. This may seem counter-intuitive at first, particularly in this book, primarily because chapter two makes a sound case that both long-term loyalty and career stability are fast-fading remnants of 20th-century work. However, the fact that they are fading doesn't make them bad, to begin with. On the contrary, they defined the core principles of employment for several generations before the current one. The actual reason loyalty and career horizons are shrinking is due to the high degree of dishonesty with which they have been implemented.

Once an implicit promise is routinely broken by both employers and employees, the very concept of an employment guarantee becomes meaningless. There is simply no trust left, though trust can be rebuilt. With strategic talent, this is an absolute must and there are two broad ways to do so:

1. *Incentivizing long-term thinking and performance through the smart use of long-term incentives*: Performance and retention-linked compensation schemes have been very popular tools since the 1990s in managing senior management employees, but till the start of the 2010 decade, they rarely went beyond vanilla stock options or restricted stock awards. They have been misused too, as we saw in the banking industry a decade ago. Incentivizing the wrong parameters drives the wrong behaviour for sure. This works the opposite way too. By using incentives smartly, and with a critical few in

the organization, we can still achieve the purpose they were meant to be for. After the 2008 banking crisis, the bankers didn't have the will to do so, so regulators on both sides of the Atlantic had to step in.

CASE STUDY: INCENTIVES DRIVE BEHAVIOUR: HOW REGULATORS CHANGED BANKING

Some of the worst banking excesses, which eventually precipitated a financial system collapse across much of the western hemisphere in 2008, could be put down to a bad incentive model. The bonus system used by market-making banks at the time largely rewarded short-term gains over long-term risk. This resulted in a sustained speculative bubble which almost sank the global economy when it burst. The ensuing global recession cost trillions, with some estimates for the US economy alone losing 22 trillion dollars in lost economic activity.[30]

In the aftermath, though, regulators forced banks to build much stronger deferred incentive programs, with strong claw-back mechanisms designed to alter executive behaviour in what had become a notoriously short-term oriented industry.

If deals made in one year did not deliver value in subsequent years, incentives tied to this deal could be retained (or clawed back), including from staff who may have retired or left the organization.

Clawbacks and penalties aren't for every industry. Moreover, I am not an advocate for punitive clauses unless they fix critical behaviour gaps. The purpose of this case study instead is to remind us how powerful a tool compensation and incentive programmes are in driving the behaviour we want from sections of our talent pools.

The reason retention incentives have proved only partially effective in the past is that they have been used indiscriminately by HR. Everyone at a senior enough level got them. The billion-dollar account winner got them, as did the HR managers themselves. However, in design, they were never meant to drive equity. They were always meant to reward only the real value creators. We don't need long-term retention plans for all internal roles—just those whom we see as balance-sheet talent.

2. *Investing in Career Management and Development*: In chapter 2, we saw how greater portability of benefits have progressively lowered loyalty and job tenures over the last three decades. A direct consequence has been the shift in responsibility for career development from the manager's shoulders to the employee. While most performance-driven organizations still see value in funding short-term, performance-linked skills development, shrinking budgets for career development are proof of the limited payback organizations see in an era of high job mobility. And while it may seem a little old-fashioned to go back to a time when career development was actively facilitated, yet in full-spectrum organizations, this is exactly the direction we must go. Not for all types of talent, just strategic talent.

Career development initiatives can be a powerful hook in the retention and engagement of strategic talent. As a balance-sheet talent, by definition, this group must see a longer career horizon within the organization than the average employee today does.

Moreover, while strategic talent may still own and drive their individual development goals, companies that prioritize funding and work flexibility to support career development efforts find it much easier to retain the key custodians of long-term revenue, relationships and intellectual property.

FUNCTIONAL INNOVATORS

The second source of internal capability deals with the organization's need for technical expertise and innovation. This includes specialized technical and functional teams and key governance roles.

Few people can credibly dispute the contribution made by functions like Finance, HR, Marketing, IT or Security to organizational success. These roles provide both necessary design of technical solutions, as well as meaningful intelligence and advice to business managers.

At the same time, the very attributes which make them valuable—depth of knowledge or focus on governance—have sometimes resulted in these functions becoming swollen and insular bureaucracies, often sorely out of touch with changing business realities. This ends up severely reducing the organization's strategic prospect and operational speed.

The real risk these largely industrial-era functions pose is their predisposition to needless complexity in both process and practice.

The HR function is a good case in point. Starting sometime in the mid-1990s, HR structures have been on an unending transformation, which has resulted in a doubling of distinct HR titles within the function. This emphasis on internal compartmentalization has today resulted in a Byzantine network of narrow expertise. What is tragic is that all this change hasn't broadened the scope of this function at all. This intricate web of HR practitioners is skilled at just one factor of organizational capability—full-time employment.

Having missed the wood for the trees, HR's skills seem overly focused on finding and keeping internal headcount, as opposed to helping govern the talent system as a whole. This internal focus has meant that the HR function today influences a shrinking slice of the organization's aggregate capability, with functions like Finance and Procurement stepping in to drive the agenda on alliances, outsourcing and external talent.

This is the true cost of HR's insular transformation. By missing the largely external trends in capability, HR today lags behind peer functions like Finance or IT in creating a transformative impact on business value.

LEAN AND MEAN

In an age of hyper-competitive digital business, any functional evolution must focus on three main outcomes:

* Simplification
* Insight through data
* Automation

Having observed how a few functions have successfully changed in the past—from administrative and clerical departments into sophisticated and strategic partners to the business—I am confident that functional transformations are the need of the hour in most major organizations. It starts with a functional leader's largely intuitive recognition that the function they will lead in the future will look very little like it does today.

From a full-spectrum perspective, functional capability is being shaped by two constituent and largely simultaneous shifts.

The first is the unquestionable shift to digital service delivery. It is now quite evident that the easiest way to deliver repetitive and menu-based services today is through self-service applications.

And the recent explosion of cost-effective and easily customizable vanilla-applications is already underlining this shift. This should result in the total and categorical automation of basic, algorithmic task delivery over the next strategy cycle. Powered by the cloud, this makes the physical location of delivery infrastructure considerably less relevant.

On the execution side, most functions are currently staffed by vast armies of low value-add executors who do little more than order-taking and vendor management, a needless cost and complexity multiplier. These roles will be the first ones to be replaced. Predominantly through digital interfaces which connect those who order services and those who deliver them.

The second shift, quite simply, is the relentless war on the average transaction cost of functional services. Increasing business disruption and market volatility don't allow for non revenue-creating services to continue being both inflexible and pricey. Lean operating philosophies driving thousands of start-ups and business turnarounds across the world are showing us exactly why this approach doesn't work anymore. A great example can be seen in how the notoriously traditional oil-and-gas industry is starting to look at unwinding its outmoded approach to inflexible functional costs.

CASE STUDY: OIL VOLATILITY AND THE TRUE COST OF FUNCTIONAL DELIVERY

The oil industry, by design, plays a very long game. Petroleum companies acquire exploration blocks decades before they start to exploit them, sometimes bidding and buying rights even before the technology to exploit the resources has been invented. Given the long time horizon underlining several business decisions, price volatility in the short term can play havoc with the industry's cost models.

There is an adage in the oil business which goes something like 'high prices hide a lot of sins'. When oil is $120 a barrel and exploration margins are robust, very few worry about marginal costs and bloat.

However, when prices fall to $25–$40 a barrel, as they have at different points, these same high fixed costs acquired during good times can be disastrous for profitability.

This invariably results in renewed interest in non revenue-linked cost structures underneath the surface, support functions being foremost among them.

Consulting major BCG finds that on an industry-wide basis, support functions—such as supply chain (logistics, warehousing, procurement, and materials management); technology (technical computing, field digitization); health, environment and safety (HES); HR; and finance—can constitute anywhere between 10 and 45 per cent of operating expense per barrel of oil equivalent (BOE) and can also contribute to escalating capital costs. Optimizing these functions can readily add one to two dollars per BOE to earnings and dramatically increase the effectiveness with which these support functions serve internal customers.[31]

Fixed cost of 10 to 45 per cent is a significant amount in a volatile price environment. Even at a low estimate of 20 per cent, these ancillary costs are a potent profitability risk. Analysis done by BCG shows that optimizing support functions can add up to $2 a barrel in saved costs. This $2 doesn't seem like much if a barrel of oil trades at $100; but what if a recessionary spell brings the price down to $30 in the future?

What is happening to the oil industry isn't all that uncommon. The industry is being disrupted through an onslaught of regulation, environment protection laws, changing consumer usage and new competition from renewables. This makes functional optimization an urgent requirement.

TECHNICAL INNOVATION

In a post-digital world, the bulk of functional task delivery will be done by self-service software, specialized vendors, highly skilled fixed-term contractors and external agencies. The few internal resources that form the fixed-cost base, hence, must be dedicated to bringing in new ideas which take the function forward in areas like process simplification and digital self-service.

This doesn't diminish the role of technical experts, particularly in the boardroom. But it does change their orientation completely— from spending the bulk of their time firefighting the technical execution challenges of today to solving the organizational challenges of tomorrow.

In dynamic-capability-speak, functional innovators are a slim remnant of the resource-intensive functional teams which populated the industrial-era organizations. As the case study about the oil industry shows, there is a strong business case to rationalize traditional functions like accounting and finance, HR, public relations and others down to just a few innovation leaders per department. These internal innovation-driven roles must exist for four main reasons:

1. Streamlining and simplifying processes for mobile application-based service delivery.
2. Speeding up execution, through self-service and automation.
3. Aligning outsourced expertise for on-demand task execution.

4. Improved governance, through data analytics and real-time reporting.

Fig. 4.4 illustrates the role functional innovators play—that of the creative and analytical brain system, which sits in between the customer application interface (on top) and the service delivery architecture (at the bottom).

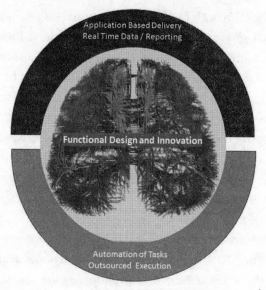

Fig. 4.4: Design and Innovation Focus within Functional Roles

In summary, it is the central and cerebral role they play that makes functional innovators as valuable as strategic talent.

DYNAMIC CAPABILITY MANAGEMENT

The third pillar of internal capability deals with our existing management talent The traditional concept of 'management' is in an existential crisis today. Mainly because traditional management processes were built for the supervision of physical work in factory environments. This is the main reason why we find knowledge workers increasingly frustrated with their supervisors, who are often seen as an impediment rather than an enabler of work. Even if these managers are well trained and well intentioned, it seems that popular management techniques of the 20th-century industrial economy are failing badly in the new world of knowledge work. There are two main reasons for this.

Firstly, the nature of supervision has changed. Instead of observing how the workers are working on a factory floor, supervisors are finding it hard to supervise knowledge work in an age where cause and consequence can be distant in time and space. With more employees engaged in cognitive tasks, often performed in front of a computer screen, supervisors have little to observe in real-time anymore.

Secondly, a major reason for the waning supremacy of supervision is the changing character of the 21st-century knowledge worker. Talent today is more aware, assertive and empowered than ever before, which makes it more responsive to coaching and facilitation as opposed to direction and control. And organization cultures are changing to reflect this need by dialling down entitlements, privileges and distinctions associated with rank. This is an age which puts a premium on democracy and respect over authority and seniority.

Consequently, I find many companies are considering doing away with managers altogether and experimenting instead with ideas like Holacracy, self-management and peer-to-peer management.

Online retailer Zappos is probably the most famous example, perhaps because its founder Tony Hsieh has always been a bit of a maverick and isn't afraid to experiment. As Tony says when underlining his support for autonomous teams and self-management at Zappos: 'Research shows that every time the size of a city doubles, innovation or productivity per resident increases by 15 per cent. However, when companies get bigger, innovation or productivity per employee generally goes down. So we're trying to figure out how to structure Zappos more like a city, and less like a bureaucratic corporation. In a city, people and businesses are self-organizing. We're trying to do the same thing by switching from a normal hierarchical structure to a system called Holacracy, which enables employees to act more like entrepreneurs and self-direct their work instead of reporting to a manager who tells them what to do.'[32]

Zappos (now part of Amazon) is a wildly successful start-up which sells shoes online, a fact that frequently prompts the argument that self-organizing and leaderless structures may be suited more to the fast-paced world of online commerce. Yet, systems which dial down or eliminate management can also succeed in more traditional environments. The most famous example by far is California-based agri-behemoth, the Morning Star Company.

CASE STUDY: THE COLLEAGUE LETTER OF UNDERSTANDING

Morning Star isn't just the largest tomato processor in the world; it is a company with billion-dollar revenues and a belief in minimal management. Its 600-strong internal talent (supported by 4,000 seasonal, temporary workers during the harvest season) don't report to any supervisor but instead, report to one another. This arrangement fosters a simple, uncluttered yet incredibly powerful and flexible system of peer-to-peer commitment. At Morning Star, job commitments are formalized when workers sign something called a CLOU (Colleague Letter of Understanding)[33] at the start of each year.

An individual's CLOU includes their mission and a list of negotiated commitments made to all colleagues impacted by that individual's work. Every sixty days, CLOU commitments are tracked and reported on by all parties involved.

No job descriptions or supervisors are needed in the system which creates a virtuous balance between responsibility and reciprocity.

Eliminating management input may work for companies like Zappos, Morning Star and perhaps hundreds like them, given the specific business models and cultures they aspire to create, but as a mainstream choice, abandoning the positives that management guidance provides would be akin to throwing the baby out with the bathwater. We don't need the hawk-eyed supervisor of the last century for sure, yet we can see the pivotal and adhesive role a more updated management culture can play within a distributed capability system.

In particular, the essential role that management can play is in helping integrate the effort across the nine different pillars of dynamic capability. We call this integrative role Dynamic Capability Management. And while there is an entire chapter at the end of the book which focuses on making a future-ready culture come alive, it might help, at this stage, to quickly review three distinct shifts in perspective needed to recast your management philosophy for a new age.

THREE PRINCIPLE SHIFTS IN DYNAMIC CAPABILITY MANAGEMENT

#1 FROM PYRAMIDS TO JIGSAW PUZZLES

A symbiotic organization needs symbiotic leaders and dynamic capability models need dynamic integrators of effort. The best way to visualize how this differs from traditional management models is to first stop picturing the future organization as a pyramid. That structure has already seen decades of flattening. Think of it instead as a set of independent jigsaw puzzles which all fit together at their edges, thereby creating a bigger and better picture in aggregate.

Junior managers are tasked with getting their pieces to work together, while more senior managers help coherently integrate several adjacent parts of the organizational jigsaw. Remember, the pieces in this jigsaw puzzle don't all just represent internal resources. The system integrates external, transient and on-demand capability just as it does headcount. Finally, imagine large parts of the puzzle representing external alliances. Whole clusters even. As strategic as they may be to the overall picture, they still need careful alignment and systemic integration with their edges locking into a coherent big picture.

Managers in such a system must be able to see how the picture comes together, including gaps which need fixing. They need to be masters of finding and cultivating capability, be it fixed roles, just-in-time talent or alliances and networks which create value. Seen in this light, dynamic capability management isn't just a skill for junior managers and team leaders. It represents a broader culture shift which touches every management position in the organization—from the CEO at one end, all the way through to the first-time leader on the other.

#2 FROM ENTRENCHED TO MOBILE

Mobile and swappable management talent, as a means of organization, represents a shift in management culture, away from linear control and direction, towards mobility, reciprocity, collaboration and the delivery of big-picture outcomes.

Fungibility, which stands for 'substitutability', basically describes a management system where managers are mobile and can be deployed on the projects which matter most to the organization. It makes management less about job titles and organization charts and more about the value a trained manager can create in the moment. Of these attributes, mobility is probably the most critical one to avoid one of the most endemic weaknesses of the industrial pyramid—managers (particularly senior ones) building entrenched and fortified fiefdoms which compete for power, influence and resources.

Although some level of hierarchy is needed, it must be transient and aligned to specific organizational outcomes. We must see this as a fundamental response to the needs of a fast-moving and disruptive digital economy.

All through the 20th century, silos and permanent hierarchies were an integral part of industrial design. As instructive parts of a viable bureaucracy, their main function was to ensure the delivery of repetitive processes, at scale. For example, imagine a factory which churned out a million homogenous products in a day. The great industrial behemoths of the time were like gigantic precision-timed machines engineered to deliver the same outcomes, repeatedly, over long durations. Though these machines were improved and tinkered with constantly, the core technology, expertise and cost architecture remained largely predictable. This time has passed.

Future-Ready Organizations are better imagined as the internet, increasingly seamless and in a constant state of evolution. The world they operate in is prone to systemic shifts, like rapid technological obsolesce, industry convergence and other forms of disruption.

From a design-thinking perspective, the successful organizations of our time must be able to respond to these often unpredictable changes more spontaneously.

This makes a dynamic capability system and management mobility as critical input factors—because ideas, innovation and experimentation all thrive around a strong core or responsive management.

#3 FROM SUPERVISION TO CURATION

The biggest shift isn't in the way we organize managers but in the very purpose of management itself. As discussed earlier in this chapter, traditional (industrial) managers primarily saw themselves as supervisors of internal performance, tasked with making headcount more productive year after year. In dynamic capability environments, their role is much more integrated into the performance of the team. Managers are the pivots around whom distributed capability gets organized. This requires them to be great project managers, sound communicators, efficient trouble-shooters and creative problem-solvers. By focusing on sourcing and creating value through distributed just-in-time internal or external capabilities, managers can have a powerful impact on organizational value.

Therefore, managers today must change from being supervisors of internal performance to being 'curators of contribution' from a distributed talent system. This change in posture emerges from the recognition that the orientation and skills needed to manage knowledge work are fundamentally different from those practised on a factory shop floor.

We see several examples of contribution curation in existence today, particularly in the relatively young IT businesses, which due to their more contemporary cultures—and corresponding lack of historical baggage—have altogether escaped traditional management errors.

Agile and Lean are two such examples. Both exemplify the manager's role as active orchestrators of customer value. Agile is a lightweight project management model which focuses on iterative project improvement and implementation. It is responsive, change-friendly and, above all, customer oriented. Similarly, Lean—which originated in the automobile industry—is also oriented towards maximizing value to the customer by making the 'value stream' as cost and time efficient as possible.

AGILE MANAGEMENT

The explosive growth of Agile as a new management philosophy is an indicator of the futility felt by new-age technology businesses with outmoded management concepts. In fast-paced design environments like software coding, managers must be able to lead both from the front and from behind. They must play a clear facilitatory and relational role and grow collaborative work teams, all the while creating ample space for talented individuals to do what they are good at doing.

The goal of Agile management is to orient all the talent at a manager's disposal towards value creating outcomes. And the philosophy itself came from a small cabal of thinkers who happened to ask the right questions, and in answering them, practically reinvented management in the IT industry.

CASE STUDY: A DISTINCTLY 21ST-CENTURY MANAGEMENT TOOLKIT

It was well below freezing on 11 February 2001 at the Snowbird ski resort in Utah, when a group of seventeen colleagues gathered together for a couple of days of skiing and freewheeling discussions on the future of software development. What had got this group together was a shared belief in collaborative work, iterative design and making software development much more responsive to changing business needs. The glue that bound them was an anathema for the dominant and rather heavyweight project management practices used in software development at the time. The rather clunky project management playbook (PMBOK) mimics more traditional business management competencies like planning, executing, controlling, reporting, risk management and stakeholder management. This makes it rather process heavy, unresponsive and often a poor fit for the dynamic and fast-paced world of IT.

The group of seventeen weren't there just by chance. Each of them was a thinker, creator or practitioner of alternative light-weight software development methodologies (like SCRUM, Adaptive Software Development, Extreme, Crystal, Feature-Driven Development and Dynamic Systems Development methodologies); they had gathered together to see if their common experiences with responsive design, self-organizing systems and customer collaboration could help create an industry standard which would minimize time while enhancing flexibility and speed. What emerged was the Agile manifesto.[34]

MANIFESTO FOR AGILE SOFTWARE DEVELOPMENT

'We are uncovering better ways of developing software by doing it and helping others do it. Through this work we have come to value:

Individuals and interactions over processes and tools
Working software over comprehensive documentation
Customer collaboration over contract negotiation
Responding to change over following a plan
That is, while there is value in the items on the right, we value the items on the left more.'

The Agile methodology is management re-imagined for the digital age. This is paradoxical because it borrowed liberally from the philosophies of the industrial age, particularly lean manufacturing, Toyota's just-in-time approaches and other new-age ways of managing more nimble and responsive manufacturing. Yet, Agile has recast industrial management models to make them more change-friendly, collaborative in nature and most importantly, put the customer rather than the process at the centre of operations.

Built around frequent delivery, iterative design and strong customer responsiveness, the Agile manifesto is operationalized through twelve principles.[35]

Twelve Principles of Agile Manifesto

1. Customer satisfaction as the highest priority.
2. A comfort with changing requirements, even late changes.
3. Frequent delivery.
4. Business and development folk must communicate daily.
5. Build around motivated individuals.
6. Ensure face-to-face conversation.
7. Working software as the primary measure of progress.
8. Achieve a sustainable pace of development.
9. Continuous attention to technical excellence.
10. Simplicity as an essential.
11. Self-organizing teams.
12. Regular reflection on effectiveness.

We find multiple customer-centric development systems commonly follow the Agile principles. Be it Scrum, with its focus on cross-functional skills, scrum masters and development work organized in fast-paced 'sprints', or Kabaan, which uses visual tools to manage multiple pipelines of work and defuses authority throughout the team, or even Extreme, which uses practices like 'pairing' (two programmers sharing the same workstation, screen and mouse) to ensure high quality problem-solving.

AGILE MOVING MAINSTREAM

When compared to old job descriptions which individualize contribution and performance, the Agile principles are better tuned for the chaos and complexity inherent in modern knowledge work. The time is right to take them beyond IT into the broader realm of business management. A good way to see the difference between the two management styles is to directly compare the job description of a traditional manager with that of a Scrum Master. Scrum methodology is highly Agile, as well as a simple and lightweight development framework very popular in the software industry.

Ken Schwaber and Jeff Sutherland, the creators of the Scrum methodology, designed a Scrum Team to include a Product Owner, the various members of a Development Team and a Scrum Master. The Scrum Team is largely self-organizing and cross-functional. In Schwaber and Sutherland's own words, 'The Scrum Master is a servant-leader for the Scrum Team and helps those outside the team understand which of their interactions with the Scrum Team are helpful and which aren't.'

How the two jobs juxtapose against each other is described in the table, 'Traditional Managers vs Scrum Masters'.

Traditional Managers vs Scrum Masters

How Traditional Managers See Their Role	How Scrum Masters See Their Role
• Identify what needs to be done • Design the division of labour • Assign tasks to individuals • Set performance standards • Keep track of what people are doing • Ensure task completion—on time and with quality. • Plan and manage budgets • Schedule and lead team meetings • Review progress against set objectives • Deliver positive and developmental feedback regularly • Coach for performance improvement • Rate an employee's performance relative to their peers	• Helping clear backlogs • Understanding product planning in an empirical environment • Enhance team agility • Facilitating Scrum events • Coaching the Development Team in self-organization and cross-functionality • Removing impediments to the Development Team's progress • Helping employees and stakeholders understand and enact Scrum and empirical product development • Causing change that increases the productivity of the Scrum Team • Working with other Scrum Masters to increase the effectiveness of Scrum in the organization

Dynamic Capability Management aligns well with the integrative and facilitative nature of Agile management because it is possible for knowledge work to be allocated to the people best suited to do it. Remember, it isn't just talent which is mobile today, the work itself is highly mobile too. Further, many digital skills are essentially platform skills and hence highly commoditized in nature.

Whatever the methodology you may choose to build or borrow, it is important to publish it and train all managers explicitly on the rules and boundaries they must now employ. Because if we agree that in the future, every organization is essentially a digital organization—enabled through digital technologies, engaging customers on digital platforms and using online applications to drive sales, engagement or compliance—then it isn't just the seamlessness of outcomes, but equally the methodology employed to deliver those outcomes which must be consistent across a large organization.

In some ways, the Agile management methodology isn't a new concept: as an example, Skunkworks was being used by Lockheed Martin as far back as the second world war. Within the twenty-year IT growth curve, Agile has now found mainstream expression across an entire industry. If it is the explosively successful IT industry *where* Agile methodologies have inarguably demonstrated a mature and responsive 21st-century way of management, it is equally *why* other industries must now sit up and notice it.

5

SOURCES OF DYNAMIC CAPABILITY
The Human Cloud

*Every once in a while, a new technology, an old problem and a
big idea turn into an innovation.*

—*Dean Kamen*
Inventor Segway

EXTERNAL CAPABILITY

While a strong core of internal talent forms the stable backbone
of every organization, an over-reliance on internal capability
is a bit like the dregs of yesterday. Because the most exciting talent
developments over the next five years won't be internal at all.
They will happen in what we now call the 'human cloud'. This
marketplace for both short and long-term external talent—which
exists alongside an AI-powered mechanical cloud (more on that
later)—promises to provide businesses unimaginable speed,
flexibility and savings.

This may sound unbelievable to a few, primarily because of subconscious attitudes towards temporary talent. In my conversations with business heads, I sometimes get glimpses of what seem to be deep-rooted prejudices towards contingent labour. Their main refrain? Can this seriously be a source of high impact talent?

Business leaders who grew up in the pre-digital era may still see hourly, project and part-time jobs as dead-end work, that is, work done by people with few other prospects—like kids on a summer break flipping burgers or delivering packages or perhaps even minimum wage work at a supermarket. This may have been true in the 1980s or 1990s, where most people had a clear preference for full-time jobs and the security and benefits they provided.

However, there has always existed a strong ecosystem of contingent talent throughout history. As an example, kings across millennia have used mercenaries to supplement their regular armies. In a more modern setting, the arts have traditionally appreciated the quality of freelance talent much more than business. Think of any Hollywood A-lister from Cary Grant to George Clooney, along with almost every other actor who works project to project. Alternatively, we could look at the highly sought-after sessions musicians, for that matter, like Tommy Tedsco, whose guitar can be heard on tracks sung by Elvis Presley on one end all the way to the Beach Boys on the other. Few know that rock god Jimmy Page was a sessions musician in England, working shift to shift for bigger names before he co-founded Led Zepplin.

THE RISE AND RISE OF CONTINGENT CAPABILITY

While the human cloud available to business today shares the same structural foundations—short-term relationships and flexible deployment—as the traditional temporary workforce, it also differs in one material way. In the modern economy, we have seen the very nature of contingent work transform—from manual work to knowledge work.

Our external capability is being rapidly reshaped by technology and automation and there are four observable trends showing us exactly how this is being done:

1. Most low-paying temporary jobs of the past are either being enhanced through mechanization or being automated.
2. Legacy blue-collar and middle-income jobs are being unpacked into individual tasks and fulfilled through a combination of robotics, algorithms and contingent talent.
3. Lean and Agile management has started codifying collective supervision of both internal and external resources.
4. A new class of labour with deep expertise has emerged forming a highly skilled human cloud.

A significant consequence of these trends is that it makes freelancing a viable first-choice career. Aided by rapidly maturing digital platforms which help them market and monetize their skills, a majority of modern independent knowledge workers today may actually prefer contingent work to full-time employment. In America for example, the annual and independently conducted 'Freelancing in America' survey (commissioned by Upwork)[36] finds that nearly two in three (62 per cent) of freelancers today make the same or more money than they did before they started freelancing—indicating that freelancing can be an even more lucrative career path than traditional jobs. In 2017, half of all freelancers in Upwork's survey felt that there was 'no amount of money' that would attract them to a traditional job. This surprised me, so I went looking for corroborating evidence and found several concurring points of view. For example, nearly nine in ten (88 per cent) from a sample of over 1,100 respondents in a similarly timed survey by Freelancer's Union said they would continue freelancing even if offered a traditional full-time job.[37]

Business perceptions towards freelance talent are slowly changing too. Upwork's data shows that 69 per cent of freelancers agree that perceptions about freelancing as a career are becoming more positive.

In practical terms, what this means is that unlike in the past, today some of the smartest and most productive talent chooses to give up the rigid strictures of full-time employment in favour of the freedom a project or a gig-based lifestyle affords them.

Freelancers aren't a small fragment of the global economy. In the US, as a case in point, the Government Accountability Office finds that just over 40 per cent of the US workforce is in some form of alternate work arrangement,[38] and one in six US workers are either independent contractors or self-employed workers.

If we broaden the scope to focus on the entire north-western hemisphere, McKinsey and Co. estimates that '162 million people in Europe and the United States—or 20 to 30 per cent of the working-age population—engage in some form of independent work'.[39] Of this number, McKinsey tells us that forty-nine million do so reluctantly, but the substantial majority, seven in ten independent workers (113 million), see it as a conscious career choice.

Mercer Consulting's data concurs with this. They found that as many as 77 per cent of full-time employees they polled across the world in 2017 would consider working on a contract basis to fulfil their needs for flexibility and enhanced control over their time.[40]

With some of the smartest talent now determined and able to monetize their capability as premium freelancers, the global contingent workforce presents the single largest talent opportunity for the modern enterprise—the ability to buy skills just-in-time rather than having to buy future potential. But this could develop into a potent solution for demand–supply imbalances in the availability of skills across industries or geography.

YOUR EXTERNAL TALENT STRATEGY

The biggest advantage of a mature external talent strategy is the speed with which external talent can help create business value. As we saw in the previous chapter, every organization still needs a core nucleus of internal employees and Balance-Sheet Talent. What it also needs in the future, more than ever, is a core network of external talent.

The smart money is on companies who are investing in mapping and mobilizing external talent, with one influential report on 2020 trends predicting 'more than 80 per cent of large corporations planning to substantially increase their use of a flexible workforce'.[41]

Your external talent strategy should focus ruthlessly on capability areas which involve:

1. *Non-perennial jobs*: Even those that demand deep expertise. Some common examples being forensic accountants, auditors in finance, compensation-and-benefits professionals in HR, lawyers, architects and hundreds of similar job groups which are subject to seasonal or irregular demand. It doesn't make sense blocking full-time headcounts in roles where their impact ebbs and flows. Besides, when made full-time, we force expensive talent to invent work just to look busy throughout the year. It is also a fact that full-time jobs in these areas often attract mediocre talent willing to accept long patches of low-impact dormancy.
2. *Surge demand*: External talent can be a powerful and immediate enabler of growth, particularly in times of sale

spikes, new product launches, geography-specific growth, seasonal demand or business-critical projects. I once spotted a project which dragged on for two long years because it involved large volumes of data gathering and analysis upfront, which was practically impossible for the four-member project team to do. No one in the project team or management had realized that the entire project could have been completed within three months if they had hired twelve or so externals for thirty days when the initial mountain of data needed to be crunched.

3. *Marginal assistance*: If the Pareto Principle applies to team productivity, then 20 per cent of the time invested produces 80 per cent of the results. The balance time (80 per cent) is normally consumed by routine process and bureaucracy. Smart job redesign can help externalize much of this. As an example, when I recently set up a securities trading account with a bank, the relationship manager I initially met was clearly an expert, who answered all my queries and ensured my risk profile and account qualifications were mapped in our first meeting. I was pleasantly surprised when he tasked an external agent to coach me through the substantial paperwork I needed to submit before the account could be opened. I never met this agent, who worked with me exclusively over email and telephone. Scanning and organizing submissions took multiple days and a fair bit of paperwork going back and forth, but it was a system which worked. The busy and expensive relationship manager focused on what he did best, and the agency which supported him was patient, committed and digitally equipped to see the deal through, without me having to leave the office even once.

4. *Deep Expertise*: In professions operating at a blistering pace of innovation and change, existing experts can often

fall behind the industry learning curve. This is where contingent talent can be quite useful. For example, over the last ten years, there has been a sharp uptick in the use of deep subject matter experts as part-time and adjunct faculty on college campuses. This, in turn, is disrupting the centuries-old professorial tenure system, which just hasn't proven nimble enough to meet the demands of either students or their future employers.

5. *Hot skills*: Several companies are finding it difficult to find, hire and retain skills which are in prodigious demand. We can see this in the mining and oil industries, which frequently run short of geologists, or in online retail, gaming and analytics firms, where an acute shortage of data scientists and data architects ends up holding back R&D or product decisions.

6. *Commoditized work*: Technology platforms which farm out simple, repetitive or algorithmic tasks to a large global pool of ready talent, are driving an 'Uberization' of several business services, from medical record keeping to multimedia design and legal services. As an example, a rudimentary search for 'legal services' on freelancer site Guru.com reveals over 22,000 freelancers offering everything from the drafting of simple contracts all the way to preparing a plaint for litigation.

7. *Technology enabled tasks*: These are traditional jobs which have been redesigned through significant automation. Consider how software accounting packages have changed the bookkeeper's job, or how digital calendars, email, voicemail and instant messaging have disrupted secretarial services. In such tasks today, it is quite easy to add on-demand human support through inexpensive freelancers. This could be a virtual assistant or in my case, a virtual finance manager who

maintains and compiles my company's statutory accounts at a fraction of the cost of a full-time executive.

These seven forms of contingent work described above can be easily done using the Dynamic Capability Framework. The framework itself divides all external talent into three broad clusters (fig. 5.1).

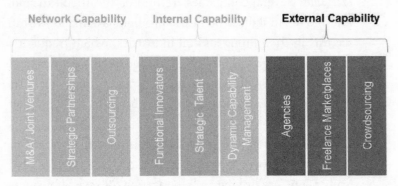

Fig. 5.1: External Talent Structure

AGENCIES FOR PREMIUM TALENT

Some of the best talent in the market today is not in employment. They are sharpening their saw, designing breakthrough solutions to emerging problems, working for multiple companies and as a result, earning rock-star status within their peer communities.

This isn't a new phenomenon. Agencies have always been a rich source of contingent talent. Think of the thousands of law firms, accounting and audit practices or advertising agencies which have existed for ages. Most start as small collectives, with a few partners coming together before some grow into behemoths, rivalling their biggest clients.

As a Dynamic Capability source, agencies could be big or small, old school partnerships or new technology-driven marketplaces. They all qualify, as long as they meet two key attributes:

1. Agency talents are professionals with niche capabilities of deep expertise which has been tested and validated or certified.
2. Their price (cost per hour) is significantly higher when compared to more commoditized external talent.

In IT, as an example, agency talent comes from the top 5 per cent or so in a key domain and could command thousands of dollars in consulting and troubleshooting fees. Many have achieved pre-eminent status or tall ratings by winning highly visible competitions. Others have achieved high reputation scores on sites like Stack Overflow. Still others go through an intermediary like Toptal, who vets and approves their skills.

The media is awash with stories of coders quitting jobs at Google and other marquee technology firms to earn more while Freelancing. As Bloomberg reports, 'Amid an accelerating war for tech talent, big companies and start-ups alike are paying top dollar—as much as US$1,000 an hour, according to a person who gets coders' work—for freelancers with the right combination of skills. While companies still recruit many of the best minds, they are turning to independent software developers to get a stalled project going, or to gain a competitive edge. In some cases, the right person can be the difference between a failed and a successful product.'[42]

Sites like Toptal, Crossover, 10X, Crew and Scalable Path (and others like them) are gold-mines for clients looking for urgent professional support. As networks of highly accomplished or top contingent talent, they invest in pre-selecting or vetting the talent they offer. Toptal for example only accepts candidates into its talent pool after they pass interviews, technical exams and a live demonstration of skill in a test-project environment.

Because agencies deal in premium talent at higher rates than most freelance marketplaces, it's easy to find high-quality people with specific strengths or even middle management capability through them. With these sites to support them, many individuals have quit full-time jobs in favour of the flexibility and diversity of contingent work.

The real benefit of using this channel is in the time saved. Rather than taking months to fill a role, most of these sites can help you find someone who could become operational in a matter of days. There are safety nets too. For example, Crossover allows you to integrate a real-life work simulation as part of your screening process, while Toptal offers a free no-risk trial period for every engagement.

THE SUPER TEMP

Another stream of agency talent includes a global network of highly skilled senior executives available for short contractual assignments. Popularly called the 'Super Temp', they are accomplished managers who help plug gaps in middle and senior management or functional roles. Within the rapidly ageing workforces of countries like Japan, Korea, Europe and North America, we have a mushrooming crowd of early or post-retirement executives who still have a lot to contribute. In their fifties and sixties, they have several good years left and valuable career experiences to offer. LinkedIn is probably the best place to find an experienced freelance executive. Many of them are willing to work at a huge discount when compared to what they may have earned in the past.

To serve this market, several sites working as intermediaries are springing up too, which focus exclusively on the Super Temp or high-end management contractor. The biggest is probably Business Talent Group (BTG), which claims 30 per cent of the Fortune 100 companies as customers and over 5,000 vetted managers on their database. BTG has tens of competitors too. Expert360 offers 15,000 preselected management contractors. Talmix boasts of 25,000 vetted management temps in over a hundred specialities and in 150 countries.

This talent isn't inexpensive, with daily fees running into mid-three-figures before the agency bolts on a 10–25 per cent fee. Yet the relative value could be priceless, especially if an important project is bottlenecked due to a lack of short-term management, unforeseen departures or the urgent need for narrow domain expertise not available internally. On this last point specifically, there are several agencies today which offer Super Temps and technical talent in narrower niches. This can be particularly useful to companies looking for immediate access to a narrow band of hyper-specialized skills. Yourencore, for example, has 11,000 experts with an average twenty-five years of experience, but specializes in just three areas—biopharma, consumer goods and medical diagnostics. Others like Wahve specialize in insurance, while still others offer talent from a common source, a good example being the Cincinnati Consulting Consortium (CCC). Started by a large group of ex-P&G executives, CCC offers sixty consultants in areas like purchasing, branding, consumer insight and innovation, with proven P&G pedigree. Consider how valuable this could prove to smaller companies in the FMCG world, looking to borrow and learn from a brand leader.

Probably the most exciting innovations in agency talent can be found in the micro-consulting world. Here, companies like the Gerson Learman Group (GLG), Alphasights, Third Bridge and Coleman Research are playing the role of high-end aggregators. These four firms have together collected the top 2 per cent of industry thought-leaders and made them available on an hourly or daily basis through their websites. Moreover, as they grow—GLG alone is already valued at over a billion dollars—they could give traditional industry firms like McKinsey or BCG a real run for their money. Micro consulting differs from the other agency sources in some material ways. For one, this is a knowledge source, as opposed to a talent source. With fees ranging from $400 to $2,500 an hour, it may prove too expensive to contract their talent for long-term assignments. A majority of consultations last between forty-five minutes and a couple of hours. Most are done over the telephone, video conference, short face-to-face interviews or on the side-lines of industry summits.

Agency talent presents some of the best opportunities for organizations to supplement internal capability through high quality, tested, external skills. For short-term projects, filling knowledge gaps, looking for cutting-edge solutions through a hackathon or premier contest, or plugging an unexpected hole with bridge talent, a robust pool of agency talent and a well-thought-out strategy could be a business lifesaver.

FREELANCE MARKETPLACES

Before we examine the life of a pure-play freelancer, it may be useful to acknowledge that there are no hard boundaries between a lower-end agency worker and a pure-play gig worker. The whole spectrum of external capability sits on a loose continuum, which could look like fig. 5.2.

$2,500 an hour	$100 an hour	$15 an hour
Super-agents	Freelancer	Micro-tasker
(Data Scientist)	(App Designer)	(Uber Driver)

Fig. 5.2: Spectrum of External Capability

Hence, given the shapeless constitution and evolutionary nature of the human cloud and the platforms which enable it, we must be prepared to encounter more than a few overlaps.

There are material differences between all three sources of external capability. Agency talent normally possesses deep domain mastery, is significantly costlier, and largely paid for time (per hour or per day). This limits agency talent to the best consultants, management contractors, thought leaders, lawyers, media professionals and the companies that represent them.

Freelance marketplaces operate at a cost rung (or two) below premium agency talent. These marketplaces are vast in comparison, with numbers running into several million skilled experts, but have remained relatively invisible to traditional organizations till recently. Because they don't resemble anything the world has ever seen before, they tend to appear quite puzzling to the uninitiated.

Yet, this is a group at the very heart of the human cloud, which holds the potential to, one day, disrupt employment itself, influencing everything including job and task design, time-based compensation and perhaps the very concept of work itself.

Such a big evolution in employment has few precedents. However, there is one that does stand out. The human cloud rivals what Henry Ford did to manufacturing a century ago with the introduction of the 'integrated moving assembly line'.

CASE STUDY: DISRUPTING MANUFACTURING, THE FORD WAY

Henry Ford was forty years old when he incorporated the Ford Motor Company, forty-five when he launched the iconic Model T automobile, and exactly fifty when he revolutionized manufacturing forever.

When Ford's Model T was introduced in 1908, it followed the same manufacturing process of its predecessor, the Model N. A team of workers laid out all the individual parts on the floor and dragged a single chassis on skids, as they went about assembling and completing a car.

However, Ford himself was fascinated by the continuous-flow processes used by the meat industry and flour mills at the time. Keen to experiment, he began by breaking up Model T's manufacture into eighty-four distinct steps and training his workers to each master just a single step. Eighty-four experts now built a single car and both productivity and quality improved.

This emboldened Ford to go even further and in December 1913, he unveiled his first automated and integrated 'moving-chassis' assembly line, with a single chassis moving slowly down a powered conveyor—from the frame to the finished car.

The innovation proved so powerful that it took the manufacturing time of the Model T from an already efficient 12.5 hour per unit down to 90 minutes!

Over the next twenty years, we are likely to see advances in machine intelligence integrated with a vast and mature human cloud do something similar to the unpacking and reallocation of knowledge work. It is difficult to predict the world that will emerge on the other side, though I for one do not see full-time employment surviving as the only or default career option.

I say this because job design activities during the industrial age ended up clumping multiple tasks together into 'employable units'. We know this today as the ubiquitous 'job-description', against which talent is contracted, assessed and compensated. But what if a job description could be 'unpacked' and reorganized, like Henry Ford did at his factory? Could this help talent build deeper expertise on the specific tasks they do best?

The best talent has started recognizing this intuitively. The question they seem to ask is—Instead of spending a large percentage of available time on peripheral tasks, can I do just one or two things distinctively well and build a career doing just so? The answer, the data tells us, seems to be a resounding yes. A great contemporary example can be seen in the data science industry. Where the attraction of solving real-life problems—along with the ability to continuously test and sharpen skills—is already drawing some of the hottest talent towards contingent work.

'MY CAREER IS A MULTIPLAYER GAME'

Topcoder is one of the world's premier sites for top-drawer technology talent. Founded in 2001, the site now boasts over one million technologists on its crowdsourced platform, including data professionals numbering somewhere in the tens of thousands. What attracts them to the San Francisco-headquartered global community isn't just the opportunity to pitch for projects from NASA or Hewlett-Packard, it is also the ability to continuously learn, and benchmark their rapidly evolving skills. As one gaming geek who splits time between paid contests and fantasy warcraft describes it, 'Work, to me, is the ultimate online multiplayer game.'

Topcoder's founder Jack Hughes is a huge chess enthusiast, and the site uses a methodology modelled on the ELO world chess rankings to rank every developer, designer and data professional. The Topcoder team hosts fortnightly fun competitions called Single Round Matches (SRMs), which test skills in real-time, within various categories of data science, machine learning, dynamic programming and so on. Winners get cash prizes and add to their rating points, receive feedback and have other Topcoders peer-review their work.

Topcoder isn't the only such site. Competitors like HackerRank also use gamification, competitions (called 'CodeSprints') and award badges for accomplishment. HackerRank's million-strong coding community is probably one of the best places to look for technology talent today. So much so that technology titans like Google and Facebook are building similar platforms. Google hosts regular 'Code Jams' and launched its 'AI Challenge' in 2010. Not to be outdone, Facebook launched its own 'Hacker Cup' in 2011.

All this isn't just happening in technology. Media, arts, fashion are all transforming into vibrant marketplaces for talent. Creative marketplace Tongal uses similar crowdsourced competition to source marketing and creative content from an army of freelancers and production houses. Both marketing directors and advertising agencies use Tongal's 12,000-strong creatives community, making it a powerhouse in an age of social marketing and a potent weapon in an industry constantly searching for the next quick and topical Twitter or Instagram campaign to go viral.

Quite symbolically, during the initial ideation phase of any project, concepts must be submitted in 140 characters or less.

Tongal's revenue at US$40 million might not seem much, but it has grown six-fold in three years. More importantly, Tongal is profitable, making it a poster-child of Clayton M. Christensen's concept of disruptive innovation. It burst upon the scene in 2009 as a fully online enabler of low budget, low complexity work that no top agency would want to touch. Contrast that with their client list in 2017. Johnson and Johnson now use Tongal for over twenty of its brands. P&G, Unilever, Lego and General Motors use them too. 'Tongal is redefining the content model,' said Catherine Balsam-Schwarber, Chief Content Officer of toymaker Mattel, which in 2016, signed a two-year deal with Tongal which includes the creation of entertainment series and new toy franchises.[43]

Marketplaces are democratizing creative industries well beyond the advertising business primarily by removing boundaries between independent artists and buyers of creative content. For example, Talenthouse offers a 7,00,000-strong army of graphic artists, animators, photographers, musicians, film-makers and fashion designers in one place. For those looking for video content, MOFILM has over 10,000 writers, producers and directors in its film-making community, and Filmwallahs, a democratized collaborative for movie-making talent founded in Asia by writer and publisher Zafar Anjum, uses machine learning to 'codify the wisdom of a movie-maker'.

COMMODITIZATION OF WORK

Topcoder, Tongal or HackerRank can attract the very cream of talent, and many freelancers working through them now report six-figure dollar incomes. For low complexity project-based work, freelance marketplaces like Upwork, Gigster, Toptal or Freelancer are better suited. They are brilliant at connecting you instantly to talent, give you a variety of options to choose from and facilitate the entire transaction, including holding money in escrow till the client signs off on a deliverable.

What I love about the range of talent on these sites is that it gives me the opportunity to break down whole projects into individual tasks so that I can commission simultaneous tasks at a fraction of a single employee's total cost. As an example, a few years ago, my consulting firm had three teams working on a new community website we were launching. One team anchored the website design and functionality, while another built a content repository and the third designed our assessment engine. What would have been a six-month sequential build for an in-house design team, ended up going live in just forty-five days.

Research shows that we weren't the only ones to experience the speed of freelance project work. Research firm Forrester, in a study commissioned by Topcoder,[44] found that projects completed in nine months internally were being completed in just three when handed out to external talent. That's a 300 per cent productivity jump in just project management terms, before we even begin to consider the value these deliverables provide to the organization by coming online earlier.

A MICRO BUSINESS REVIVAL

The rise of freelance work has also led to an impressive small business revival on both sides of the skills transactions. Small and Medium Enterprises (SMEs) are ideal customers for freelance talent, especially for creative, project or commission-based work. Using external experts for transitory work allows a small business to punch well above their weight, without adding expensive overheads. SMEs, hence, are big buyers of highly skilled, short-term talent on freelance marketplaces like Freelancer or Upwork.

At the same time, the access and scale that freelance marketplaces provide have led to a spurt of micro-enterprises on the sell side, forming mini-agencies which bring together talent with complementary skills. These small businesses, that can have anywhere from two to fifty employees, can go after more complicated projects, which may be well beyond the scope of an individual freelancer. Many micro-business owners were once freelancers themselves who have gone on to build the business infrastructure to now employ others.

After years of pain for small businesses who have seen large industrial corporations eat up more and more of their customer share, the revival of small business in the world of digital freelancing is a great sign for the future.

Made up of over 150 million individual freelancers, the human cloud represents a new breed of technology natives who are redefining century-old descriptions of both task and technique. Operating at price-points the big corporations cannot match, the micro-business industry is a huge enabler of the human cloud. And their numbers aren't small. In the US, industry research places the number of freelance business owners at just under three million.

CROWDSOURCING

Besides the freelance contractors described earlier, the human cloud also has a significant chunk of micro-taskers. Companies like Uber, Airbnb, eBay, Fiverr, Flipkart and Amazon have built entire business models around this demographic. These companies see themselves as platforms, aiming to connect millions of small-ticket buyers and sellers in real-time. And their success in doing so has, in turn, led to one of the most exciting business innovations of the 21st century—crowdsourcing.

A micro-task is best described as a task which is simple, repetitive or highly algorithmic in nature. Each executed task lasts between a few minutes to a few hours, and this short life-cycle ensures that a task can be contracted, completed and paid for expeditiously, often within the transaction window itself.

For low complexity knowledge work—bite-sized jobs typically completed by a single digital-tasker or by hundreds working independently at the same time—we now have access to millions of freelancers through crowdsourced job sites like Amazon Mechanical Turk, RapidWorkers, Damongo, MicroWorkers or ShortTask. These sites, which employ mainly temporary jobbers and work-from-home talent, are ideal for quick-turnaround jobs like meta-research, data entry, basic design, and so on. Their impact is growing, with several of the top sites offering close to a million taskers at a time.

Although they live on the same continuum, it is the transaction timeframe which largely distinguishes freelance marketplaces from crowdsourcing. In other words, while the two-week design job for a database is the ideal kind of project to give a freelance designer, organizing your expense receipts or transcribing an audio clip would be something a micro-tasker could do in hours for you.

When used correctly, micro-tasking can be a powerful accelerator of personal or team performance. One example is Zirtual.com which supplies dedicated virtual assistants to subscribers, yet is priced on an hourly basis. Users buy a set number of hours per month which can be used as and when required. The dedicated Zirtual assistant, available over phone, text or email, can prove a boon to entrepreneurs and small businesses owners, who need no more than four to six hours of dedicated micro-task support per week. Speedlancer.com is another website I have been watching closely. This site tries to bring the benefits of a preselected agency-like task-force to clients, at micro-task speeds. Speedlancer promises a four-hour turnaround on tasks and integrates into collaboration platforms such as Slack so that project managers can use it as an on-demand resource.

I have found the greatest benefit of micro-tasking in the overnight turnaround. Over the last couple of years, I have sometimes sent tasks to jobbers in a different time zone, purely because I want it done by the time I return to my desk in the morning. These could be simple things like fixing fonts and graphics in a research deck, updating web-links on a content database, or even transcribing an interview while I was writing this book.

What we now know is that the global mobility of micro-tasks is helping bring work and prosperity to new regions and lifting entire communities out of poverty. A great example can be found in the following case.

CASE STUDY: CROWDSOURCING AS A FORCE FOR GOOD

Samasource is a crowdsourcing collaborative which helps take vast quantities of their client's unstructured data and organize it in a manner that makes it more valuable and useful. This includes data processing solutions such as image annotation, data classification or simple data digitization. These kinds of jobs typically sit in the crowdsourcing sweet-spot, because they are simple, low complexity and require nothing more than basic computing skills.

What Samasource does isn't unique in itself. Indeed, hundreds of crowdsourcing sites offer similar services. What is unique is *how* they do it. Located in some of the poorest regions of the world, Sama has helped pull thousands out of poverty and given hundreds of disaffected women and youth new careers, while generating impressive revenues. They manage this through what Sama calls *impact sourcing*, defined by them as 'hiring people from the bottom of the pyramid to complete digital work'.

Of the 8,000-odd people that Samasource has employed since 2008 in countries like Kenya, Uganda, India and Haiti, many have never worked before. So the founders have built in deep upfront training in digital literacy and communication, backed up by strong quality control and project management tools. With clients like Google, eBay and Walmart, it is quite clear the Samasource experiment is working.

Crowdsourcing has the potential to significantly help differently-abled talent too. The World Bank estimates that there are currently close to a billion people[45] (or a full 15 per cent of the world's population) who live with some form of a disability. Of this number, approximately a fifth, or between 110 million and 190 million people, have a serious physical or mental disability which fundamentally impairs their life and productivity.

With most unable to hold full-time and even regular part-time work, imagine if a significant portion of this 190 million demographic could find new expression in the global talent marketplace using micro-jobs. There are four main reasons why crowdsourcing can bringing millions of differently-abled talent from the margins into productive work.

1. *Flexibility*: Unlike a month-long project that a freelancer would typically take on, micro-tasks finish within a few hours. This allows talent to pick the days they work on, or even the opportunity to log-in, complete a few tasks and log-out. It could also help with medication schedules or other similar constraints which limit the amount of time available for (or even the frequency of) part-time work.

2. *Mobility*: There is rarely a commute required in digital micro-tasking, or even an office, for that matter. Taskers can be equally productive working off a kitchen table. Operating from home allows the tasker to work in familiar surroundings and the use of special accessibility hardware or software. This can prove critical for those suffering from conditions like social anxiety or those still recovering from serious physical or mental health episodes.

3. *Pace*: Because crowdsourcing unpacks complex outcomes and assigns them simultaneously to hundreds of taskers, the pace of work is fully flexible. For example, tasks like image annotation or data classification could take an expert sorter just a few seconds to complete, but be as effective when done at a slower pace.

4. *Relative Anonymity*: A freelancer is under no compulsion to declare a disability at all. As long as the work gets done, anyone can use micro-tasking to monetize capability. The relative anonymity a digital platform provides could be especially empowering to the differently-abled. Imagine a visually impaired singer operating from a home studio using Domingo or Fiverr to sell voice-overs and backing vocals.

Be it Samasource pulling people out of poverty, or millions of differently-abled talent gaining financial independence for the first time, micro-tasking is a fast-growing proposition which promises to truly flatten the earth for talent. For we are entering a world where the only legitimate borders for talent are skill boundaries.

WELL BEYOND UBER

While it is true that Uber was the one that put crowdsourced talent models on the venture capitalist's map, it was by no means the digital flagbearer for crowdsourcing.

Linux, Wikipedia, Mozilla, TripAdvisor and many similar ventures have been perfecting the art of virtual talent communities since their inception. Most of these early efforts were anchored around a nucleus of highly motivated hobbyists—experts who shared their knowledge and talent for free, purely because they believed deeply in the project idea.

Today, while Uber gets most of the crowdsourcing press, there are equally huge experiments in motion. This channel often works best when the work is low complexity and urgent, yet requires an element of technical or technological dexterity. When these conditions are met, crowdsourced businesses end up establishing entire talent systems across previously disorganized labour markets. One such example is Care.com.

Started by Sheila Lirio Marcelo in 2007, when she could not find quality care for her child and ill father, Care.com now has a staggering $160 million in revenue. After going public in 2014, the firm now has over thirteen million caregivers across Europe, North America and Australia, offering services like housekeeping, child or senior or pet care and tutoring (fig. 5.3).

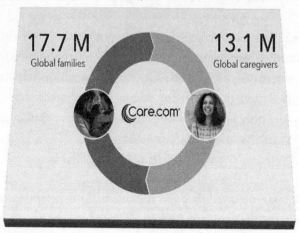

Image courtesy: Care.com Investor Relations
Fig. 5.3: Care.com

The network Care.com creates is organizing what has always been an unregulated and chaotic marketplace. Families who use the services benefit immensely because every caregiver receives background checks, past reviews and ratings.

The caregiver benefits too. In 2017 for example, Care.com pegs the average rate for their babysitting services at just under $14 an hour, a rise of 26 per cent over 2010.[46] Even the most inexpensive US location across the Care network paid $11.81 per hour on average, well above the $7.25 minimum wage.

I find traditional business can learn a lot from the crowdsourced sharing economy. Companies like Uber, Airbnb and Mozilla are geniuses at talent aggregation, allowing thousands to partner with them.

The five principles they follow are simple:

1. Get lots of people interested in the organization.
2. Lower the traditional threshold of entry. Allow people to engage based on just a few threshold qualifications, that is, a slim set of core non-negotiables.
3. Use technology to anchor the entire work transaction, and use data and metrics to show people how they are performing in real time.
4. Give people the freedom of choice. Reward commitment but don't penalize the need for flexibility. Allow talent to keep the entrepreneurial spirit alive.
5. Let customer ratings decide who the best and brightest are. Reward the best and perhaps even hire them to train others. Your future strategic and management talent could well come from the very cream of your contract workforce.

The three channels I've described provide a range of alternatives for time and cost-efficient contingent contributions. As this market matures, it shouldn't surprise us to see contingent capability become the default choice for certain sectors or skills. The plug-and-play nature and compelling cost ratios make this source of talent too seductive to ignore.

Data shows that the more progressive businesses are already harnessing the power of external talent. According to the IBM Centre for Applied Insights' exhaustive Business Tech Trends study covering over 1,500 companies,[47] the organizations that excelled at the early adoption of new technology were also the best at engaging external talent. Writing about these pacesetters, the name IBM gave to this group of outperformers, it said, 'Partnering isn't just about skills; it's much deeper and more pervasive. They're engaging less conventional partners like citizen developers, clients, start-ups and academia to help drive innovation. They're twice as likely to enlist academia to help with product development, and 70 per cent more likely to use start-ups for project execution.'

6

SOURCES OF DYNAMIC
CAPABILITY
Network Capability

Alone we can do so little; together we can do so much.

—*Helen Keller*

The last structural source of capability available to modern organizations comes from institutional arrangements, that is, organizations choosing to work together formally or informally to multiply value for both parties.

Institutional partnerships are a natural response to rising complexity and risk. The meteoric rise of outsourcing, strategic partnerships, mergers and acquisitions are just some of the observable consequences of a new and powerful network effect in global business. Globalization has also been a keen driver of alliances and joint ventures. Increasing global convergence has meant that executives looking for global scale, speed or cost efficiency today see institutional arrangements as a key component of growth strategy.

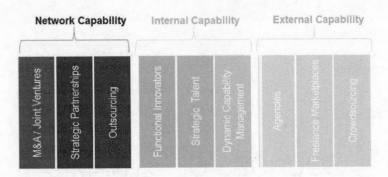

Fig. 6.1: Network Structure

Network Capability (fig. 6.1) grows from strategic collaboration. This is great for business because teamwork allows us to chase goals well beyond our reach. When used effectively, an organization's network capability allows it to chase a suite of strategic win-win outcomes.

1. Network capabilities allow for rapid increases in scale for both the organizations involved. If the relationship is truly complementary, a partnership can multiply the reach of both partners. An example of this multiplier effect can be seen in the partnership Google's Android operating system has with brands like Samsung, Huawei or Oppo.
2. Enhanced credibility through deep alliances with large and stable partners.
3. Entry into new markets. Joint ventures and strategic partnerships are great ways to test new markets before making any investment in organic growth. This can also help access non-traditional customers and distribution networks for existing products.
4. Better brand recall due to synergetic marketing. For example, the French bank BNP Paribas is synonymous with

the game of tennis through its multi-year sponsorship of ATP (Association of Tennis Professionals) events.

5. The increasingly common practice of innovation sourcing involves large organizations buying smaller start-ups for their innovative products and ideas.

6. Streamlining an organization by eliminating non-core activities. In practice, this is what the outsourcing industry has grown from.

7. Sharing of market or distribution risk, particularly when growing globally or going after new customer segments, or managing complexity, be it in regulatory risk, compliance, logistics or distribution.

8. Commoditizing and packaging of tasks, mainly to drive down costs through outsourcing and similar arrangements.

9. Sharing costs, particularly in large projects or when developing new markets.

10. Talent sourcing through the increasingly popular practice of 'acquiring' (buying out a smaller company for its talent).

While the basic ethos of network arrangements are mainly complementary capabilities which result in mutual benefits, there are three broad types of network arrangements in common use.

1. *Capital Deployed*: These are long-term arrangements which reside on the balance sheet. They represent investments made in strategic capability acquisition, the most popular being joint ventures, franchises, acquisitions and mergers.

2. *No Capital Deployed*: These are contractual arrangements for the short or medium term which do not involve a financial investment, for example, strategic partnerships, brand alliances, cooperatives and the like.

3. *Vendor relationships*: These are medium to long-term contractual arrangements which reside in the profit-and-loss account. For example, a purchase of services on the client's end and revenue for services sold at the vendor's end. The most popular example is outsourcing.

Let's examine each in some detail.

MERGERS & ACQUISITIONS / JOINT VENTURES
and other capitalized structures

Relationships requiring capital investments, by definition, reside on the balance sheet. They are invariably medium to long-term arrangements too, and they are becoming very popular strategic plays in business today.

THE RISE OF M&A

Let's start with mergers-and-acquisitions (M&A), which mostly happen due to financial or market share considerations. Boards looking to enhance share value or protect market share, often use them to achieve economies of scale, or alternatively, to build a bigger moat against current and future competition.

Mergers are often a consequence of industry consolidation, a phase when industry-level changes such as technology shifts or geopolitical trends reshape the competitor landscape. The mega airline mergers in the USA during the 2000s are an example of this. After struggling for years in tough competitive environments, the first phase of consolidation started when TWA and American Airlines were merged in 2001. This was followed by merger of US Airways and America West in 2005, Delta with Northwest in 2008,

United with Continental in 2010 and finally, American Airlines once again with US Air in 2013.

Today, M&A activity outstrips new IPOs by some margin and has led to unprecedented shrinkages in publicly traded companies. The number of listed US companies peaked at 7,562 some time during the summer of 1998. By 2015, this number was down to 3,812, and today, according to the Wilshire 5000, the number is just over 3,500.[48]

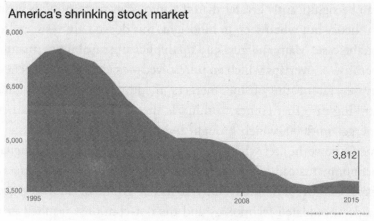

Source: CNN Money / Wilshire Analytics
Fig. 6.2: Stock Market Shrinkage

A big reason for this shrinkage (fig. 6.2) in publicly traded stocks is the spike in delistings brought about by a booming M&A market. According to Deallogic,[49] a record $5 trillion worth of deals took place in 2015, with ten M&A transactions each worth a massive $50 billion or more. These numbers are unprecedented. Compare this number with new companies going public. In all of 2014, across the US, $96 billion was raised by 282 new public companies. At the peak of the IPO market in 1996, the number of new companies at 848 was three times that number. This shows us how the global M&A market has matured over the past decade.

This isn't happening by chance. In an age where half of the companies in the hallowed Fortune 500 list in 2000 have now disappeared from the list, the ownership patterns above could show us how both entrepreneurs and investors are recalibrating for a new age of mammoth disruption.

GREATER THAN THE SUM OF ITS PARTS

M&As happen when both sides are convinced that the new whole can be significantly greater than the sum of its parts. Sounds great in theory but when seen in hindsight, this doesn't always seem to be the case. Many mergers end up duplicating capabilities, mainly because of overlaps which go unresolved—exactly what happened in several of the airline mergers mentioned earlier. Another striking case that comes to mind is the AOL and Time Warner merger in 2000, which brought together dominant internet and media powerhouses which were in the nascent stages of the digital economy. Instead of becoming the industry-shaping force many expected the combined entity to be, a group of short-sighted leaders, outdated technology and the dot-com bust resulted in a colossal $100 billion loss barely three years later.

In theory, while the term merger implies the coming together of two equals, this is rarely the case in practice. All mergers have a dominant partner of sorts, and it is this dominant partner's culture that provides the roots from which the new, combined entity grows. Ignoring this fact, or even tiptoeing around it, are fatal mistakes.

M&A AS CAPABILITY STRATEGY

When used effectively, though, mergers can be powerful tools to bring together complementary capability. By resolving overlaps swiftly and decisively restructuring with an eye on new opportunities, mergers can reshape entire industries. Probably the best example of this comes from the merger between Disney and Pixar in 2006, which has resulted in some of the highest grossing movies of all time. A key reason this happened was that Disney (the acquirer), had the maturity to recognize the strong complementary capabilities Pixar possessed.

CASE STUDY: WHAT DISNEY AND PIXAR TEACH US

When Disney bought Pixar in 2006, it was the logical next step in what had been a very successful partnership. Together, the two partners had collaborated on mega-hit movies like *Toy Story 1* and *2*, *Finding Nemo* and *The Incredibles*.

It was Disney's new head, Robert Iger, who was able to convince Pixar (and major shareholder Steve Jobs) that merging the companies would be the best way to save the partnership from going stale. However, it was a risky deal. For one, the price they settled at in 2006—US$7.4 Billion in Disney stock—looked outrageously high. Further, it would make Jobs Disney's biggest shareholder, with a stake of close to 7 per cent, an outcome which was difficult to justify given Pixar owned a lean library of just six animated features. Analysts were quick to draw parallels to Viacom's 2005 acquisition of DreamWorks SKG for US$ 1.6 billion, which included DreamWorks library of 59 films.[50]

It wasn't just content which was being valued here. As Roy Disney Jr said at the time, 'Animation has always been the heart and soul of the Walt Disney Company and it is wonderful to Bob Iger and the company to embrace that heritage by bringing the outstanding animation talent of the Pixar team back into the fold.'

Consider for a moment what this meant to Disney, who after a golden run for decades, had seen its internal animation studios put out a series of average earners like *Brother Bear* (2003) and *Chicken Little* (2005).

The Pixar merger was primarily about Disney ringfencing the best animation capability within the industry. It also formed an alliance which would go on to deliver billion-dollar hits like *Toy Story 3* and *Finding Dory*, not to mention lucrative downstream merchandizing and income from Disney theme park attractions.

Capability-driven mergers can create enormous value. Another great example can be seen in how Proctor and Gamble and Gillette amplified each other's capabilities after their merger in 2005. P&G was a global marketing and distribution powerhouse while Gillette possessed a peerless innovation pedigree with market-leading products. The merger was such a resounding success for both parties that it might just have caused a significant shift in behaviour. Many today prefer the acquisition route over in-house R&D as the cornerstone of their innovation strategy.

ACQUISITIONS ARE THE NEW R&D

A generation ago, in more linear and predictable times, research and development (R&D) was an exclusively internal activity. Many organizations invested significant chunks of money in running large innovation laboratories with hundreds of products in different stages of development. Beyond the R&D department, universities were the other hotbed of innovation. Academia supervised and helped generate patents by the thousands, and good universities had strong and competent technology transfer offices which oversaw the commercialization and licensing of new intellectual property.

The stories of true garage-based innovation were few and far between. As much as we venerate the Apple Computers story as a true example of frugal innovation, the reality is that it happened rarely. The main issue almost always was a serious lack of funding. Most micro-entrepreneurs struggled to get the early capital to develop an idea, as we saw in the Steve Jobs and Nolan Bushnell case at the start of this book too. This situation invariably left many smart innovators with tons of great ideas with two main options:

1. Get an expensive bank loan by putting everything on the line. Or,
2. Find an R&D job in the well-funded product laboratory of a major corporation.

There were no other options.

The seismic rise of venture capital has upturned the entire R&D philosophy within industry. So much so that both internal and academic R&D are currently in shambles. As Forbes magazine reported in the summer of 2014, 'Of the 2.1 million active patents, 95 per cent fail to be licensed or commercialized. These unlicensed patents include over 50,000 high-quality patented inventions developed by universities.'[51] Recent reports suggest that the vast majority of technology transfer offices aren't even earning enough to cover their own administrative costs.[52]

Internal R&D can be risky too, as accountants will tell you. It consumes large amounts of precious retained earnings. It is often hit-and-miss—big projects reach nowhere and there is no guarantee of payback at all. And finally, the bureaucracy and lethargy baked into big business unnecessarily stretches out the time and cost it takes to bring a new idea to market.

It is for this reason that acquisitions of small and mid-size start-ups have become the route of choice for big businesses looking for blue-sky innovation. It is safer and relatively cheaper to acquire an idea once it has already demonstrated commercial value. It looks better on the books too. As compared to R&D expenses which eat into profits, acquisition cost is generally capitalized. The icing on the financial cake is the incremental revenues and new customers the start-up brings.

The pharmaceutical business is a good example, where data from the Tufts Center for the Study of Drug Development suggests that getting a new prescription drug to market now takes close to a decade and costs $2.5 billion.[53] For companies with lagging internal innovation prospects, often an acquisition is the only way out. We see the same behaviour in the technology business too, where companies like Alphabet, Facebook, IBM and Microsoft buy up tens of start-ups a year for their innovative products or ideas. Some go on to attain greater importance in years to come, as YouTube proved at Google or WhatsApp proved at Facebook. Yet a large majority of the acquisitions get subsumed into existing products, or simply disappear due to a poor strategic fit.

There is a clear trend in modern business—internal R&D works best when improving existing products, and acquisitions of start-ups are the preferred avenue for blue-sky innovation. However, there is a middle path too, a hybrid approach that incorporates benefits of both. Moreover, for some, it demonstrates a more systemic commitment to distributed and outside-in innovation. For example, in 2006, looking to counter the runaway success of Airbnb, Accor, the French hotel chain, bought a 30 per cent stake in private rental company Oasis. Oasis's inventory of curated rental apartments with upscale services like a dedicated concierge and guest lounges could now be booked through Accor's global booking system.

Others don't put in capital upfront but run popular accelerators to incubate fresh ideas. In Asia, Target's India operation runs a four-month accelerator for local retail start-ups at their Bengaluru campus. PepsiCo runs competitions on eYeka as part of its Pepsico10 idea incubator. Nike runs a three-month Nike+ accelerator in Portland, Oregon to incubate digital sports innovation. And they aren't the only ones doing this. Almost all of Nike's key competitors have similar experiments underway.

JOINT VENTURES

Joint ventures (JV) are among the smartest capital-investment strategies to grow a global business. And while they aren't the hottest trend of the season like innovation focused acquisitions are, the sheer volume of joint-venture activity over two decades of globalization has fortuitously left us with a mountain of evidence on how JVs can be used to fuel growth.

In essence, joint ventures are shared ownership structures where two or more parties come together to share expertise and risk. As a capability structure, they are ideal tools in a couple of specific situations. They work best when:

1. An organization is looking to unlock value from an urgent and immediate opportunity. For example, when one organization with a deep product or technological expertise wants to access customers in a new market. In such case, a deeply entrenched local partner, with consumer insight, regulatory standing or expertise and an established distributor network, could prove an ideal partner. A joint venture gives both partners oversight over investments and

strategy. This has been the preferred approach for global companies looking to gain a foothold in emerging markets like China in the 1990s or Africa today.

2. Two or more mature organizations want to collaborate on an opportunity but want to give their partnership a level of operational autonomy. While risk and return is still shared by both, a joint venture helps create an independent entity which can be governed and managed professionally. One example is ViiV Healthcare, an HIV focused joint venture between GlaxoSmithKline (GSK) and other partners. GSK and Pfizer came together in 2009 to establish ViiV, with both partners transferring their existing HIV research and other relevant assets to the new company. In 2012, Japanese drug-maker Shionogi also joined the JV as a third co-owner.

The biggest risk to joint ventures, and indeed the reason they sometimes fail, is when partner organizations end up at cross purposes. Invariably, these structures face challenges and adverse operational realities, as all organizations do. If both 'co-venturers' are committed to cordially working through issues while protecting the common ground, then the joint venture itself may end up stronger and more resilient.

STRATEGIC PARTNERSHIPS
and Other Off Balance-Sheet Alliances

The second source of network capability are organizational relationships where capital isn't deployed. And while this makes them looser and more flexible arrangements, it also makes them more responsive and collaborative. The sweet-spot for strategic partnerships exists in areas of complementary capability. As a result, these partnerships work perfectly with products and services which operate either upstream or downstream to yours.

The key to successful strategic partnerships are situations where:

1. The collaboration sweet-spots vastly outnumber the competitive overlaps.
2. They enhance the customer's experience or value.

In other words, in deep and complementary partnerships, sales origination doesn't matter, because for the customer, buying a joint solution is much better than negotiating with each partner independently. Mature customer-centric partnerships recognize that if coming together helps enhance the customer's advantage, then collaboration serves the interest of all the parties involved in the transaction.

Let's see how both factors work in practice. Imagine an industry with five dominant players, each offering differentiated products. We could illustrate their opportunities and overlaps as in fig. 6.3.

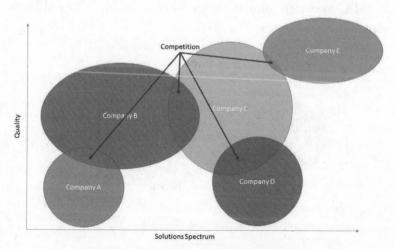

Fig. 6.3: Collaboration and Competition

On the surface, all five firms compete with one another. This competition is good and helps expand the number of options available to a customer. However, in areas where firms are not in direct competition, or for customers looking to consume a broad spectrum of services within this industry, there exist significant opportunities to collaborate too (fig. 6.4).

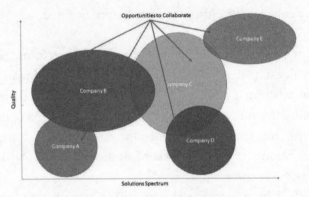

Fig. 6.4: Opportunities to Collaborate

It might make absolute sense in this example for Company B and C to design joint solutions when a customer's need looks something like fig. 6.5.

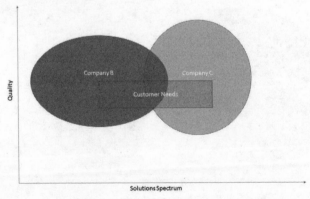

Fig. 6.5: Joint Solution: Customer's Need

This is exactly what we see in the case of Cisco Systems and Netapp, who have forged an industry-defining and wildly successful long-term partnership.

CASE STUDY: FLEXPOD

Cisco Systems is the undisputed 800-pound gorilla of the networking business, yet delivering a state-of-the-art data centre solution—either on-premises or in the cloud—depends equally on both networking and storage. Therefore, it makes sense for Cisco to offer pre-designed and integrated solutions which ease implementation headaches for the customer. Enter California-based data storage company Netapp. Together, the Cisco-Netapp partnership has implemented hundreds of unified data management solution since they decided to work together in 2003.

Their leading joint product is 'Flexpod', a pre-designed data centre solution which seamlessly integrates Cisco and NetApp's technologies. What makes Flexpod a great example of a true partnership product isn't just that it amalgamates Cisco servers and switches with NetApp storage, but as NetApp explains, each component has been built by two independent companies using the same 'fundamental theories in their architectures'.[54] Rather than rigid, this makes their products modular and flexible in use and deployment.

That's a great approach to build a true partnership because it serves the needs of a common customer. Cisco and Netapp do have overlapping products, so they compete in some areas, yet both have chosen to see the big picture from the customer's point of view.

INNOVATION PARTNERSHIPS

External collaborations also allow organizations rapid access to new capability, new ideas or even new geography. If done correctly, strategic partnerships can prove to be entry tickets to untapped markets, or they can even invent new markets through joint innovation. Here are three leading examples of how innovation partnerships can work:

1. Luxottica, the Italian eyewear manufacturer, and Google collaborated in late 2014 to produce the next version of Google Glass—the internet-connected spectacles first launched by Google earlier that year. For Google, it allowed its technology to be paired with more conventional forms of eyewear, such as Luxottica's mega-brands like Rayban and Oakley. For Luxottica, it presented an opportunity to reinvent the spectacle for the future and create a technology-enhanced product for its customers.

2. Mass-market Swedish retailer H&M has in the past successfully collaborated with designers like Karl Lagerfeld and Alexander Wang to offer some of their most successful limited-edition lines. At first, what looks like a match made in hell, that is, a high priest of fashion coming together with a mass-market clothing company, has often turned out to be a smash hit for both partners.

   For the designer, it presents an opportunity to go beyond their traditional audience and reach consumers previously locked out by price. For the retailer, the publicity and social media buzz fuelled by the designer's name ends up in long lines of people queueing up the night before launch.

3. Even Apple, probably one of the most introverted and secretive companies, successfully partnered with

MasterCard when launching Apple Pay. A major win-win, this partnership gave Apple a strong platform of existing MasterCard users and an opportunity to work with a dedicated partner to resolve teething issues. MasterCard crucially gained from the distinct head-start on the platform, before Apple allowed other card companies like Visa and American Express on it.

These aren't isolated examples but reflect a broader trend. The best organizations increasingly use alliances to grow or innovate. So much so that the very nature of future business is collaborative. IBM's Business Tech Trends study I referred at the very end of chapter 5 says that pacesetting organizations were also exponentially better at external collaboration and partnerships. According to IBM, 'Partnering is integral to how Pacesetters plan and execute. Across every type of external partner and for every type of activity we examined, Pacesetters partner more. They also partner more creatively, recruiting less traditional partners for their efforts.'[55]

OUTSOURCING

Outsourcing is probably the most mature source of network capability across the network capability spectrum. Not only have we been outsourcing work from one company to another for centuries, but the last fifty years have seen an outsourcing boom of sorts. As things stand, outsourced business-to-business (B2B) relationships today—covering both manufactured goods and services—make this multi-trillion-dollar industry the bedrock of the global economy.

Today, every medium or large enterprise outsources in some shape or form. The cost and competitive dynamics of modern industry force us to do so. And the industry has matured dramatically as a result. Long accused as a ploy to drive down costs, we have started seeing more examples today of outsourcing as a means to enhance quality, or even scale beyond what can be achieved internally.

The credit of this shift from cost to quality can go directly to two great management thinkers—C.K. Prahalad and Gary Hamel.

Coimbatore Krishnarao Prahalad was born in a small town in south India in the years preceding the country's independence from the British. A brilliant student and alumnus of the Indian Institute of Management in Ahmedabad, Prahalad was teaching business strategy at the University of Michigan when he met Gary Hamel.

Hamel, a young doctoral student at the time, went on to collaborate with Prahalad and in 1990, the pair published a breakthrough article in the *Harvard Business Review*. The article was called 'The Core Competence of the Corporation'. The success of their ideas soon inspired them to write their celebrated 1994 book, *Competing for the Future*.

Their hypothesis was a simple yet compelling one. Hidden within the complex web of capabilities an organization possesses are 'core' and 'non-core' organizational competencies. Prahalad and Hamel described core competencies as those fulfilling three specific provisions—'They provide potential access to a wide variety of markets, make a contribution to the customer benefits of the product, and are difficult for competitors to imitate.'[56] Through the process of selection, whatever is left is non-core which, while important, does not directly contribute to a company's competitive advantage. The two academics implored managers to refocus the purpose, strategy and resources of the organization towards these core competencies, and in doing so, structure the residual 'non-core' tasks to be done in the most cost and process-efficient way as possible.

The proposition was a powerful one. Executives spent much of the 1980s and early 1990s following Michael Hammers playbook, which, as we saw in chapter 2, was about restructuring the organization to drive down cost and enhance productivity. However, restructuring results had been mixed at best. Prahalad and Hamel's insight showed exactly why. Indiscriminate restructuring of a core competence could actually weaken a company's competitive positioning.

The rise of core competence in management consciousness coincided with the rise of outsourcing as a capability choice. Why did a company need an army of payroll and benefits administrators or security guards when these tasks made little impact on the customer? These roles were commoditized and often the same in every company where they were performed. Couldn't someone else do them better and cheaper? Could they become someone else's core competence?

OUTSOURCING AS A CORE CAPABILITY STRATEGY

The evidence shows that since 1990, when the trend turned into a tsunami, outsourcing has been a huge enabler of organizational growth. Peaking alongside the growth of globalization, it has helped companies refocus internal resources on higher value-add roles, such as product innovations or market expansion. What this has meant is that revenue growth has far outstripped headcount increases.

At the same time, the outsourcing industry itself has also matured by leaps and bounds over the last quarter of a century. It has grown from being a tool for cost and process efficiency to an indispensable partner of an organization's overall strategy. The set of choices which led to the single most successful consumer product since the turn of the millennium shows us exactly how.

CASE STUDY: IT'S NOT JUST WAGE ARBITRAGE

At a dinner with the US President in 2011, Steve Jobs was asked a rather direct question on outsourcing by his host, Barak Obama, 'What would it take to manufacture the iPhone in the US?'

Steve Job's answer, according to another guest at the dinner was, 'The jobs aren't coming back.'

It wasn't just about the cost. The human cost of manufacturing high-end electronics isn't as big a deal breaker as one would think. Some analysts have calculated the wage differential between China and the US at the time was a well-surmountable $65 per device.[57]

So what was it? The sheer scale and size of global manufacturing and services make some locations better suited to the work being done. In China's case, the steady migrations of hundreds of millions from rural China to industrial towns on the coast provided the numbers for large-scale manufacturing. Another distinct advantage was the numbers of engineers passing out of Chinese universities.

As Charles Duhigg and Keith Bradsher wrote in the *New York Times*, a 'critical advantage for Apple was that China provided engineers at a scale the United States could not match. Apple's executives had estimated that about 8,700 industrial engineers would be needed to oversee and guide the 200,000 assembly line workers eventually involved in manufacturing iPhones. The company analysts had forecast it would take as long as nine months to find that many qualified engineers in the United States. In China, it took 15 days.'

We see the same economies of scale available in other outsourcing locations too, be they millions of programmers available in the Indian cities of Bengaluru and Hyderabad, or long lines of customer representatives willing to work the graveyard shift across Metro Manila.

MORE THAN A VENDOR

Outsourcers traditionally have been looked at as vendors delivering commoditized solutions. But in the services industry at least, this is rapidly changing. The gradual blurring of industry boundaries between IT companies and outsourced service providers has meant that it is now the outsourcing vendors who often possess a clear edge in emerging technologies over their clients.

This shift has, in turn, changed the fundamental nature of outsourcing from cost-efficient process delivery into an opportunity to fundamentally transform the process itself. And I have seen this first hand.

In the early half of my career, which coincided with the big services push to Asia, I helped two large American organizations build large captive (owned by the company) and third-party (pure-play outsourced) service centres in India, the Philippines, Malaysia and China. The greatest challenge we faced during those five years (starting 2001) wasn't filling thousands of training seats a month in red-hot job markets or even making the venture deliver a gross margin within the first year of operation. Instead, our biggest challenges were overcoming the adversarial relationship between the client and the service provider. Outsourcing was an emotional issue for clients back then, invariably because it coincided with job losses.

To compound matters, service delivery levels were initially quite poor. In hindsight, both the client and outsourced partner were to blame. Clients often saw outsourcing as a quick-fix solution for poor processes and service providers—keen to acquire new customers—weren't investing in the due diligence required to spot slapdash systems before inking a contract. The natural outcome was several downstream change requests. Enough burnt fingers later, both sides did eventually realize that outsourcing broken or outdated methods was a shortcut to chaos, conflict and lost opportunities.

For outsourcers, climbing up the value ladder from executors to becoming process redesigners and automation experts has been an existential response. Currently, very few leading companies in contract manufacturing or services are pure-play outsourcers. They are at the cutting edge of promising developments in robotics, natural language processing, machine learning and cognitive computing. The scale they operate at affords them this R&D agenda and the freedom to drive huge efficiency by blending human workforces and intelligent automation.

The evidence is all around us. Be it Apple supplier Foxconn replacing 60,000 workers with robots at a Kunshan facility[58] or Robotic Process Automation transforming the low-end work of India's 3.5 million strong IT workforce. Some forecasts peg the loss of low complexity work (think data entry, application testing or transcriptions) at nearly half a million jobs in India by 2021.[59]

Companies must now look to outsourcers to fundamentally transform processes, either through the better use of data, cloud infrastructure or intelligent automation. The relationship now relies on a foundation of shared process innovation. It is rare to see this happen when two organizations share a client-vendor relationship in which the vendor is subservient and acquiesces to and operates through old measures like Key Performance Indicators (KPI) and Service Level Agreements (SLA).

While these measures do underpin daily operations, they mustn't be the forces driving outsourced capability within full spectrum organizations.

In conclusion, the nine sources of human capability described in this part of the book show us that an organization's capability agenda is increasingly less about your status in the company, the colour of your identity card, words in your contract or the job title you carry, and more about the value you create. In the next chapter, we take this awareness one step further by reviewing how artificial intelligence and intelligent machines are set to emerge as an indispensable tenth source of capability within the Dynamic Capability Spectrum.

7

THE TENTH SOURCE
Intelligent Automation

The real problem is not whether machines think but whether men do.

—*B.F. Skinner*

In previous chapters, we covered nine emerging sources of human capability. This chapter aims to go one step further. It focuses on the inevitable influence that intelligent machines will have on an organization's capability systems. And with all the anxiety surrounding artificial intelligence (AI), let's start with the big question which is on almost everyone's lips:

WILL JOBS SURVIVE?

The short answer is a resounding yes. The alarmist rhetoric around technology and jobs being a zero-sum game isn't a new one. It has been a constant refrain over three centuries—since the time of the earliest steam engine.

And it even fooled the most revered economist of our age, John Maynard Keynes, who upon seeing the considerable productivity gains and rapid industrialization brought about by early assembly lines, had this to say as far back as 1930, 'We are being afflicted with a new disease of which some readers may not have heard the name, but of which they will hear a great deal in the years to come, namely, *technological unemployment*.'[60]

Keynes wasn't the only one to be fooled. Humankind's ability to harness and respond to advances in technology has been written off several times in the past. In famous episode, the great Nobel prize-winning economist Wassily Leontief observed that just as the advent of the railroad and motor car eventually made the horse redundant as a beast of burden, humans would be replaced by machines too. Leontief famously suggested in 1952, 'Labour will become less and less important. . . . More and more workers will be replaced by machines. I do not see that new industries can employ everybody who wants a job.'

And yet, they were all wrong. The evidence shows that each wave of technological disruption has, in consequence, significantly enhanced human competence rather than diminished it. And while it is true that technological breakthroughs invariably reshape and transform *how* work is done, where Leontief and the others erred was in writing off the human response to technological shifts. Unlike horses, who could not adapt, human intellect and ingenuity always discovers new ways to add value, over and above what a machine can do. Probably the best industry-level example can be seen in how (in what is now becoming a familiar pattern) the finance profession responded to the advent of the first computer spreadsheets in 1983.

CASE STUDY: THE FIRST SPREADSHEETS

In 1983, with the release and wild success of spreadsheets like Visicalc and Lotus 1-2-3, many pundits predicted that we would soon have no perceptible need for general accounting and finance professionals. The convincing reasoning at the time pointed to a spreadsheet's breakthrough ability to manage vast volumes of basic financial data, calculate using preset formulae and generate reports at the click of a button. Something which took the accountants and bookkeepers of the day over a week to do manually. These new programs were more accurate too, and cost a fraction of what an expensive bookkeeper did.

This reasoning did indeed have some legs, and as the *Wall Street Journal*'s Greg Ip[61] explains, thirty-year job data from 1983 shows that jobs in the US for bookkeepers and accounting clerks did steadily decline due to the widespread adoption of Lotus 1-2-3 and the introduction of Microsoft Excel in 1987.

But there was more than a silver lining. Over the same thirty-year period, the new analytical prowess of the spreadsheet helped create several *new* roles which never existed before.

As the illustration below shows, the increase in analytical power afforded by spreadsheets and similar data management software has resulted in whole new professions—from investment analysts to forensic accountants, professional auditors, management analysts and data researchers. These roles—all of which were relied on the computational strength of spreadsheets—have resulted in human talent adding more value to the business than ever imagined. Consequently, hiring in these new roles has boomed, as a direct result (fig. 7.1).

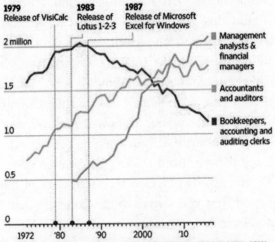

The Spreadsheet Apocalypse, Revisited
Jobs in bookkeeping plummeted after the introduction of spreadsheet software, but jobs in accounting and analysis took off.

Image courtesy: The Wall Street Journal[62]
Fig. 7.1: Spreadsheet and Jobs

Each of these professions today do miles more than their counterparts in 1983 ever did.

As the case study shows, this never-ending competition between humans and machine is best seen as a healthy and necessary rivalry, as it creates opportunities for both to improve. If one draws a parallel from sports, the greatest tennis player in history, Roger Federer, once said that he didn't feel he would have been as good or as successful in his career if it wasn't for his bruising rivalry with his arch nemesis Rafael Nadal. Like great champions, they share a deep respect for each other and warm camaraderie, purely because they see competition as a healthy and positive motivator.[63]

Two economists, Daron Acemoğlu and Pascual Restrepo, recently found this was the case not just in accounting but in hundreds of other professions as well. As they wrote in their seminal 2016 working paper on the subject, 'The dynamics of modern labour markets in advanced economies is being characterized by a race between two technological forces: automation on the side of machines, and the creation of new complex tasks on the side of man. While automation is an ongoing process which, all else equal, takes jobs away from labour, the creation of new complex tasks is also an ongoing process which adds new jobs for labour.'[64] Acemoğlu and Restrepo arrived at this conclusion after studying job creation over twenty-seven years across 330 US occupations. And they are absolutely correct.

The data shows that in the eighty-odd years since Keynes raised the prospect of 'technological unemployment', average per-capita productivity—the economic contribution of the average worker per year—in the United States has grown six times.

Machines have made labour more efficient. What Keynes got right was how automation has made almost every 1930s job redundant today. What he got wrong, though, was not factoring in the enormous growth in employment driven directly by the human response to automation. Today, we also have more jobs than we have ever had, including a vast majority which never existed in 1930.

At a systemic level, we are wrong to look at enhances in automation as adversarial to humans. There are some tasks machines can do much better, thereby freeing up time for human beings to focus on the things they do better than machines.

This is exactly what an early pioneer of AI believed. Smart automation can help humankind go beyond the natural limits of the human mind by denying us the opportunity to 'satisfice'.

SATISFICING

Herbert Simon is considered an early groundbreaker in the fields of AI and cognitive psychology. A winner of the Turing award in 1975 and the Nobel Prize for economics in 1978, it is his 1957 concept of 'bounded rationality'[65] which best explains how technology works to enhance human decision-making.

In simple terms, what Simon's theory, which successfully challenged what traditional economists believed as true, put forward was the following—our rational decision-making is, in practice, severely restricted by three factors:

1. The amount of information we have access to.
2. The time it takes us to assimilate all the information needed to make a perfect decision.
3. The cognitive limits of the human mind, that is, the mental capacity to process all this information within the time available.

'In an information-rich world, the wealth of information means a dearth of something else: a scarcity of whatever it is that information consumes. What information consumes is rather obvious: it consumes the attention of its recipients. Hence a wealth of information creates a poverty of attention and a need to allocate that attention efficiently among the overabundance of information sources that might consume it.'

—Herbert A. Simon[66]

Image Source: Herbert A. Simon—Biographical. NobelPrize.org. Nobel Media AB 2019. Fri. 1 Feb 2019.

As these factors affect the quality of all our daily decisions in a material way, human beings have become good at what Simon calls 'satisficing'. A blend of two words, 'satisfy' and 'suffice', the term implies our tendency to seek 'good enough' outcomes, as compared to the best one. And applications of Simon's research clearly demonstrate why human beings often make highly irrational decisions—often with a clear conscience—which can have calamitous consequences further down the road. We can see this all around us in the modern life. A good example can be seen in the millions of hiring decisions made each day, all across the globe.

SATISFICING IN ACTION: THE RECRUITER'S DILEMMA

The way we currently select talent through rounds of resume screening and selection interviews is a great example of how our tendency to satisfice often results in risky hit-or-miss decisions.

Let's begin with screening. A first-level screener reviews a two-page curriculum vitae, usually in a matter of minutes, before shortlisting a candidate for an interview. At that moment, those two pages represent the entire human being to the screener.

Even if the limited data available is but a tiny fraction of the information needed to make a great screening choice, a shortlist or reject decision must be triggered. Hence, the screener is forced to seek out a 'good enough' outcome, as opposed to the best one, that is, he or she is forced to satisfice. And with scarcely an afterthought that somewhere in the rejected pile may lie a potential superstar.

Interviews are just the same. If all we have is sixty minutes to evaluate a candidate, a decision must be triggered by the limited data received within that time. Even if we cannot conclusively evaluate a person's competence or fit for the job at hand. It is not surprising, therefore, to hear interviewers confess about subconsciously deciding to hire or reject a candidate within the first few minutes. Often based on vague and fluffy criteria like physical appearance or personal likeability, even though these attributes have scant correlation with competence or future performance.

This is satisficing in action. We continue to persist with a broken hiring process, having known for decades that interviews are probably only as effective as tossing a coin. As Jason Dana explains in a recent *New York Times*[67] article, 'In 1979, for example, the Texas Legislature required the University of Texas Medical School at Houston to increase its incoming class size by 50 students late in the season. The additional 50 students that the school admitted had reached the interview phase of the application process but initially, following their interviews, were rejected. A team of researchers later found that these students did just as well as their other classmates in terms of attrition, academic performance, clinical performance (which involves rapport with patients and supervisors) and honours earned. The judgment of the interviewers, in other words, added *nothing of relevance* to the admissions process.'

Fortunately, satisficing is easy to fix. With regards to the hiring process for example, in the final chapters which focus on 'how to' build a Future-Ready Organization, we see how some companies have transformed the selection process simply by delaying human decision-making. They have been able to demonstrate radical selection success simply by inserting a 'technical screen' before the human one. In most cases, this involves replacing subjective screening of resumes, which are prone to satisficing behaviours, with a scenario-based test or an upfront performance challenge, designed to delay human decision-making till a candidate has an opportunity to demonstrate competence.

The relationship between humans and machines is better imagined as a partnership with machines employed to do work too repetitive or rudimentary for human intelligence, too dangerous for human well-being or too complex for human time. Human capability, on the other hand, has always excelled at fashioning such machines, creating meaning from the unfamiliar and in imaginative pursuits. In such an arrangement, technology does replace human effort, but only in areas where human effort is suboptimal.

Well beyond hiring, satisficing influences almost all areas of management—from reviewing performance, to assessments of future potential or deciding a discretionary bonus. Perfect logic applied on insufficient information in limited time almost always results in a flawed decision.

In summary, Acemoğlu and Restrepo describe the relationship between human talent and automation as a competition. Looking at the future from Simon's perspective, though, we recognize that while human talent is best suited for some types of work, it is equally unsuited, sometimes even ineffectual, at others.

I prefer Simon's view. As we can well observe all around us, it would be hard for human beings to survive entirely without automated help, and no machine is entirely independent of human direction. Yet work is forever moving between the two. And we see this happening continuously within our internal, external and network capability.

DISRUPTING THE HUMAN
CAPABILITY SPECTRUM

The very nature of dynamic capability thinking is collaborative. Taking it one step beyond human capability involves embracing both human and automated contributions. A principal reason that a vibrant gig economy even exists today is due to web-enabled communication and collaboration. The same is true for outsourcing too. The entire industry for transnational services outsourcing grew from a standing start in 1990 due to advances in telephony, software and data mobility. It stands to reason that this trend will continue and with it the reshaping of human contribution by technology will also grow exponentially. Of the nine sources of human capability within the dynamic capability framework, there are five that will be totally reshaped by technology over the next ten years. These are given in the next illustration (fig. 7.2).

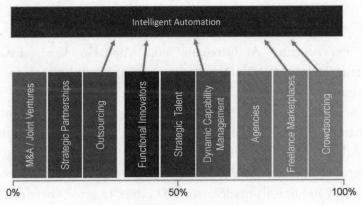

Fig. 7.2: Intelligent Automation

We know this because in each of them, the core disruptive triggers are already in motion. Let's examine eight predictions of how the human–machine partnership can reshape how we organize work over the coming decade.

1. *Machines will dominate repetitive and rule-based work. Humans will shine at creative and non-linear pursuits.*

   Key technology: Robotic Process Automation (RPA)

RPA generally refers to the automation of rule-based and algorithmic work using software. By and large, these robots are dumb—they must be programmed, turned on and provided with instructions. Still, RPA has the potential to totally transform the transactional outsourcing industry by 2030. One level above RPA sits Intelligent Process Automation (IPA), which while still rules-based, now involves a level of machine learning or 'intelligence'. This could mean a program autonomously reaching out to a parallel system, or maybe even a human, for additional information.

2. *Intelligent Machines will raise human intellect and productivity to new levels.*
    Key technology: Artificial Intelligence (AI)

Experimental AI programs like AlphaGo have already demonstrated how programs can learn complex games to eventually outperform the best human champions. It came to a head in 1997, when the Deep Blue computer beat the world champion Gary Kasparov at chess. We are discovering AI's potential by the day. Recently, an improved version of AlphaGo, AlphaGo Zero, took just three days to learn the complex Go game from scratch and beat its predecessor 100 games to zero. These events have provided new impetus and learning directions for both game designers and players. In other words, machines can teach us to go beyond presently-known boundaries of human potential. Go players are already relearning a thousand-year-old game according to Alphago Zero's patterns of play.

As opposed to dumb robots, AI relies on a level of machine learning which makes the system self-aware and capable of rational reasoning. It does so by mimicking a neural network, processing options and the consequences of those options. This is what Simon believed AI's true potential to be. Could AI programs one day be seen as a source for human learning—with an ultimate aim to improve human decision-making and eventually the human mind itself?

3. *Machines will program directly for us.*
   Key technology: Natural Language Processing

Laboratory programs today can already recognize handwriting almost as well as humans do and describe the contents of pictures, diagrams and schematics at astonishing levels of detail. The key tipping point seems to be in natural language processing, which allows software to understand and interpret human speech in multiple languages, an advance which could allow computers to write code one day and lead to the complete obsolescence of programming languages such as Java.

4. *The human cloud will exist within a much larger mechanical cloud.*
   Key technology: Natural Language Generation

The next step to Natural Language Processing is Natural Language Generation, or a machine's ability to interpret and write commentary on data independently. It is here that automation starts to overlap with traditional white-collar jobs, such as journalism or data analytics. A very good example is Quill,[68] a program which writes journalistic style commentary based on underlying data. Developed by Chicago-based Narrative Science, Quill is already writing up 10–15 page reports for regulators and investors at companies like Credit Suisse and T. Rowe Price. Think of the implications in live sportscasting and security intelligence. It shouldn't surprise us that one of the investors in Quill is the Central Intelligence Agency (CIA).

When Natural Language Generation merges with other areas of cognitive computing, such as pattern recognition or self-learning systems, the future potential is unmistakable. With massive gigabytes of data available to analyze or visualize, and an internet of things (IoT) revolution on the horizon, I can imagine programs such as Quill will one day have a seat at the boardroom table, for the immediate analytical insight they can provide.

5. *Management spans-of-control will exceed a hundred times.*
    Key Technology: Smart Agents

Smart automation can help both delayer the organization as well as radically widen management impact, through the automation of old supervisory tasks like review and reporting. This frees up managerial time and also promotes greater autonomy and sense of self-direction for employees.

Once a project is scoped and agreed upon, smart agents can easily take on the task of scheduling project deadlines, aligning priorities, dependencies, communicating critical reminders and even handling escalations independently. Management can be much more interventional as a consequence and oriented towards real value-added behaviour like problem-solving and coaching for outcomes.

6. *Applications will fade to the background and be replaced by digital assistants.*
    Key Technology: In-App and Mobile Searches, Smart Agents and Chatbots

Across industry today, it is common to drive the use of self-service applications. This augers well for customers but can also lead to a huge cluttering of applications. Smartphone users' app downloads number close to 185 billion a year—each fulfilling a narrow purpose. This can be overwhelming. Most of us like how Google searches and catalogues the internet for us, yet apps don't behave in the same way. They resemble independent books on a shelf rather than a seamless web. Industry experts now suggest that Search engines could soon have the power to crawl through, parse and index data stored within an app. This makes the app itself obsolete. Once this happens, content could potentially reach the smart agent directly, without the user ever needing to download the app itself. This will result in both simplification and speed. Instead of hundreds of enterprise applications to trawl through, more and more functions will make their data compatible with virtual digital assistants, operated by voice commands and designed to meet the needs of customers or even a specific type of talent, for example, a new hire, a virtual worker operating from home, a salesperson, short-term contractor or a manager supporting a mix of internal and external talent.

In Singapore, DBS Bank's Digibank chatbot that operates across a variety of platforms including Facebook messenger, claims to resolve 82 per cent of all queries without human assistance. OCBC, another Singapore bank, has generated over 50 million in-home loan leads via its chatbot Emma.[69] Similarly, the top insurance companies are using chatbots to help their agents and financial advisors resolve client queries in real time. Customer information on claims, past premium histories or policy values are all available through what is now seen as a virtual sales assistant.

7. *Learning becomes practical, customized and just-in-time.*
Key technologies: Virtual Reality and Augmented Reality

Virtual Reality (VR) based immersive simulations have already started changing the way we learn. For example, Oculus VirtualSpeech helps improve public speaking skills by mimicking live stage experiences with responsive virtual audiences.

Augmented Reality (AR) is the next step, which involves superimposing data or images upon what we see in real life. For example, imagine workers repairing complex machinery in a remote location being able to superimpose step-by-step schematics or training manuals on the machine itself. The implications of AR all the way from school classrooms to operation theatres in hospitals can save both time and lives through just-in-time learning.

8. *Intelligent machines make humans safer at work.*
   Key Technology: Intelligent wearables

In an Internet of Things (IoT) environment, intelligent wearables are often the smartest safety investment that companies can make, particularly in high-risk work environments. For example, Australia-based SmartCap Technologies has developed a solution which can constantly monitor operators of heavy machinery, like truck drivers, for micro-sleeps and other signs of fatigue. Similarly, wearable proximity alarm systems can help workers stay away from danger or prevent mishaps on locations as diverse as oil rigs, ship decks, underground mines and high-rise construction sites.

In conclusion, the potential for collaboration between human capability and intelligent machines is limitless and if used correctly, can transform the impact of both people and the organizations they work for. It is important that we don't see intelligent machines as the enemy, but recognize that human frailties, like our propensity to satisfice and our desire for creativity over tedium, are the real reason we need them.

ARE CUSTOMERS THE ELEVENTH SOURCE?

A possible eleventh source of Dynamic Capability is the customer. Both as individuals exhibiting distinct buying behaviours and through the terabytes of customer data now captured and available to organizations.

As customers, you and I may already work for several companies and receive fair value in return—either through superior services or free access. We are mystery auditors for TripAdvisor, photographers and content curators for Facebook or Twitter, and quality inspectors for Uber or Amazon. These companies and many others like them wouldn't be valuable or profitable if their customers weren't integrated into their capability system.

Seeing customers as talent isn't just restricted to new-age IT companies. Many traditional businesses have also successfully integrated customers deep within their decision frameworks. As A.G. Lafley, ex-Chairman and CEO of consumer goods giant P&G explains, 'Virtually every P&G office and innovation centre has consumers working inside with employees. The consumer is boss.'[70]

CUSTOMER INTIMACY

Customers today expect to have both choice and a voice in the relationship, and smart business leaders recognize this. Some companies drive engagement through a steady stream of rewards for loyalty, using things like membership points, exclusive deals, status awards or by giving altruistic meaning to customer feedback. For example, hotel rating website TripAdvisor constantly reminds its reviewers of the number of people their review has helped.

The customer voice has unprecedented power too. Social media access means that customer feedback is increasingly available to many existing and potential customers, powered by hashtags, followers and the possibility of things going viral. In addition, Twitter has given every customer a direct line to the CEO. And the best ones, like Salesforce CEO Marc Benioff or Carolyn McCall, CEO of EasyJet, really welcome the opportunity to have direct conversations with customers. There is no easier way to discover customer ideas, insights and pain-points in real time. Tony Fernandes at Air Asia showed us exactly how powerful a CEO who steps up and leads communications directly can be.

CASE STUDY: A DIRECT LINE TO THE CEO

On 28 December 2014, a routine Air Asia (QZ8501) flight from Surabaya to Singapore crashed into the Java Sea shortly after take-off. The Airbus A320 carried 162 passengers and crew. There were no survivors. Yet what surprised everyone was that from announcing the bad news to the search operation which took a week, it was the CEO Tony Fernandes who led the communications relay with the public, directly through his twitter account.

Fernandes flew to Surabaya immediately after the crash and took it upon himself to keep tweeting news at regular intervals. The tweets were a mix of factual updates, his own feelings of personal anguish and direct responses to distressed family members looking for information.

Air Asia went through hell in the months that followed the crash, but its reputation and consumer trust rebounded soon after. Unlike other airlines that have suffered irreparable brand damage from similar accidents, Fernandes's willingness to be accessible and examined in the toughest time possible, is a big reason why.

Beyond customer involvement and intimacy, it is the huge volumes of data that customers generate which make them central to our capability models. And the quality of immediate insight now available is changing the very nature of expertise.

YOUR NEW EXPERT: DATA

We have all traditionally relied on subject matter experts (SMEs) for insight. Their deep knowledge helped us make better decisions and their past experiences helped us avoid costly mistakes in the future. But expertise takes time to gather and has a shelf life. In times of rapid disruption and change, what we often realize quite painfully, is that most SMEs are actually experts on yesterday. No one is a true expert on tomorrow. Fortunately, there is a better alternative.

With more and more buyer interactions online, there is a new authority emerging—the customer. As the Chief Marketing Officer of the gaming developer Reloaded Games once explained to me, 'Today, technology has been democratized and is in the hands of the common man or woman. Core marketing strategy in the digital realm is no longer dependent on SMEs, but rather it's about simply interacting with your consumer in real time.'

In the absence of expertise, it is high-quality data which drives great decisions. I have no doubt that over the coming strategy cycle, customer intimacy, buying behaviour and deep real-time analytics will develop into a powerful eleventh source of capability, rivalling the other ten we have reviewed.

8

BUILDING THE FUTURE-READY ORGANIZATION
Dynamic Capability
Leadership

We are like islands in the sea, separate on the surface but connected in the deep.

—*William James*

The book thus far has focused on the 'why' and 'what' of dynamic capability. It has drawn a map of what is changing in the world of work and why we as organization strategists must change too.

In this part of the book, we focus exclusively on the 'how'. The goal of every chapter that follows is to empower you, as the leader, with practical ideas, approaches, frameworks and tools to bring Dynamic Capability Management to life in your business and in doing so make your organization future-ready.

We will do so by looking at the three critical ingredients needed to build a Future-Ready Organization:

1. *Dynamic Capability Leadership*: Or in other words, how the role of the business leader is transforming within future-ready organizations
2. *Dynamic Capability Management*: Which covers the specific skills needed by people managers to cultivate capability and curate contribution from a dynamic capability system
3. *Dynamic Capability Strategy*: Which gives you the tools to approach and consciously modify the capability system driving your business

There is no better place to start this execution journey than with the proverbial million-dollar question:

WHO OWNS THE TALENT AGENDA?

Any company that wants to craft a future-ready talent recipe needs a deliberate diagnostic and forecasting process to do so. The first question to answer is: who owns this effort?

Traditional thinking points us to the HR department. This is a mistake. HR's current skill-set—and toolkit—are heavily oriented towards the management of internal employment environment. HR has an important seat at the table, but cannot currently drive the non-payroll segments of your capability model.

Should it be the procurement function? That wouldn't work either. Although procurement manages vendor relationships, the skills it brings to the table are too outward-looking and cost-centric to play a lead role.

What about the finance function, then? Finance understands the economics of the talent agenda better than most and has a rich track record in the disassembly and outsourcing of both critical and non-critical tasks. This legacy's function of deep involvement in some of the fastest growing segments of the networked enterprise – mergers, acquisitions and joint ventures makes a strong case for finance. However, finance's numbers prejudice often limits its ability to see beyond dollars and cents.

I believe the answer to this question is inextricably linked, at a philosophical level, to the evolution of business itself. This is an age in which companies which gain access to the smartest talent, and possess the speed and flexibility to extract better economic value from this talent, are at a significant competitive advantage. The best vantage point to lead this effort therefore does not sit on the margins of business, that is, in support functions like finance or HR, but within the business itself. Orchestrating capability in the future is a dynamic process which must be led by the senior-most business leaders themselves. In other words, *in a limitless and global talent system, the CEO is also the Chief Capability Strategist.*

For this to happen, the organization's core talent agenda, which was incubated in HR over the last few decades, must now leave the margins and travel rapidly to the very heart of the business.

NOT AN UNPRECEDENTED JOURNEY

What this means is that the entire concept of talent needs re-imagination. Not in HR's process-driven language, but rather in the core economics of customer value.

In the annals of business evolution, this isn't an unprecedented outcome. Over the last century or so, many of the core competencies driving business today have made this very journey—from marginal functions to the organization's core. For example, it may shock many readers to learn that the customer wasn't always the king. For the vast majority of economic history—from feudalism to the mercantile age—customers had little choice and often ended up getting a raw deal. It was the rise of the free market economy in the late 19th century which increased the value of customers and placed them on par with the interests of business owners. The entire customer service revolution which was to follow can be largely put down to the efforts of a couple of path-breaking founders.

It all started, not surprisingly, in the hotel business at the turn of the 20th century. César Ritz, the legendary Swiss founder of the Ritz hotels in Paris and London, was famous for saying, '*Le client n'a jamais tort*' or 'The customer is never wrong', a philosophy that set his brand apart from all the other luxury hotels and won his business a long line of fans. As a consequence, the Ritz soon came to define a standard of hospitality an entire generation of hoteliers now aspired to.

In a dramatically similar example, a few years after the Ritz was redefining service in the hospitality industry, a store opened on 15 March 1909, in London, which would change the retail shopping business for ever. Selfridges on Oxford Street was probably the first store ever designed to make shopping a fun activity, as opposed to an inconvenient chore.

At the time, the rich never went shopping and products were rarely on display. Harry Gordon Selfridge, the far-sighted founder, didn't just want to create a place to sell things to people.[71] He wanted to give shoppers an experience which would keep them coming back. If they came more often, perhaps they would also buy some products on the side? Selfridge is also often credited as the creator of the phrase 'The customer is always right', making a positive interpretation of Ritz's maxim.

Ritz and Selfridges were two early pioneers of the customer service revolution. Others soon followed and through the first half of the last century, customer service—that once was a dusty little department which managed damaged goods and exchanges—went all the way to the heart of business. Not just in hospitality and retail, where this started, but almost every industry saw the rule-book rewritten, with the customer at the centre of it all.

Noted Harvard economist Theodore Levitt spotted this shift clearly in 1960 when, in his book *Marketing Myopia*, he stressed the need for marketing to shift from product orientation to consumer orientation. In 1974, management guru Peter Drucker indubitably endorsed this change. In his breakthrough book *Management: Tasks, Responsibilities, Practices*, Drucker wrote: 'To satisfy the customer is the mission and purpose of every business.'[72]

Tracing a similar path through the 1960s and 1970s, we also saw the quality agenda travel from the margins to the core of business.

THE DEATH OF DEFECT

We live in a world today where almost everything you buy off a supermarket shelf works. So much so that most warranties and guarantees that manufacturers give are never invoked. Such is the supremacy of present quality standards that companies not committed to product quality just don't survive any more. Their goods and services fade from consumer consciousness. This wasn't always the case. On the contrary, indifferent, and sometimes even rank bad, quality was quite the norm before the Second World War.

After the war ended, everything changed. Hard lessons learnt about the cost of poor-quality war supplies were soon being re-purposed for civilian factory shop floors. A significant milestone was laid in 1951 when Joseph Moses Juran, an American engineer, published the first edition of his *Quality Control Handbook*. It soon became the definitive bible of manufacturing quality.[73]

While Juran was busy inspiring American business, across the Pacific another American, the statistician William Edwards

Deming, along with a local university professor Kauro Ishikawa, was about to make Japan the industrial powerhouse of the 20th century. Losing the Second World War had devastated Japan's economy and Japanese products in the early 1950s were synonymous with poor quality. However, in just a couple of decades, Deming and Ishikawa built a uniquely Japanese system of Total Quality Management,[74] which involved every employee in root cause analysis and quality improvement. The Japanese quality revolution lasted thirty years and by the early 1980s Japanese engineering products were easily setting world class benchmarks for others to follow.

Juran, Ishikawa and Deming were soon followed by the ISO 9000 family of quality standards, the 'zero defect' philosophy and the Six Sigma approach pioneered by Bill Smith at Motorola. All took quality further towards the heart and purpose of business. When Jack Welch at General Electric adopted Six Sigma as a core management philosophy at the company, the quality agenda had truly arrived at the CEO's table.

FROM ANALOGUE TO DIGITAL

More recently, particularly since the start of the new millennium, we have seen information and digital technology travel in the footsteps of customer centricity and quality. While this journey is by no means complete, the huge impact it has made on business competence since 2000 has been nothing short of breathtaking.

I remember the time in the early 2000s when IT heads in traditional companies were no more than network managers. They invariably sat in ice-cold server rooms and spent most of their day adjusting ethernet cables or rebooting hardware. The only time the head of IT entered a boardroom was when the network was down and the Chairperson couldn't send an email.

Not any more. Most heads of IT today, now called Chief Technology Officers (CTOs), have pride of place at the boardroom table. CEOs recognize the competitive advantage a good CTO or CIO brings to the business and the power IT possesses to disrupt entire industries. Technology too now lives at the core.

FROM HR PROCESSES TO INTEGRATED CAPABILITY MANAGEMENT

Quite like customer service, quality and IT, the organization's talent agenda too is on a similar journey, away from HR's headcount driven monomania, towards a much broader approach in an age of blended capabilities.

The indicators of this shift are there for all of us to see, particularly in the fact that headcount numbers (as a percentage of sales) have been in decline for years. Driven by productivity increases and the technology-enabled redistribution of work, we rarely see mature organizations significantly increase employee numbers today. If anything, it is the news of mergers, restructures and lay-offs which dominate the business news.

A more significant consequence of this shift away from HR-led talent agendas can be seen in strategic outsourcing trends. Driven by globalization, we have seen tens of millions of manufacturing jobs move to countries like China, Mexico and Thailand. At the same time, countries like India, the Philippines, Hungary, Russia and Poland have claimed mighty chunks of outsourced services. If you add domestic outsourcing and the explosion in high-quality contingent work, we can see how increasing amounts of organization capability are now driven by finance, procurement and business leaders themselves.

If there is one thing that the five dynamic capability case studies in chapter three tells us, it is that every enterprise today is already a mix of all three sources of human capability—internal, external and network. As a result, we can safely say that an organization's core capability agenda has left the HR incubator and is already moving to the heart of business.

Most business heads intuitively sense this shift but lack the governance architecture to accelerate an open talent system to maturity. As a direct consequence, disconnected decisions taken by HR, finance, procurement, legal and other functions have resulted in a mishmash of tactical practices.

Is it time for a reboot? I believe it is. Given the journey that talent is on, we do seem to need new answers to new problems, rather than another retrofit of past practices. The key question is the one I began this book with, 'What's your future talent recipe?' The answer won't come from the margins (HR or procurement or finance) this time. This is a question every P&L leader must answer. *The CEO is now the Chief Capability Strategist.* In this role, there are two specific outcomes he or she must champion:

1. INTEGRATED CAPABILITY GOVERNANCE

An organization's capability recipe isn't static. It changes over time as new opportunities emerge. Hence, like any creative pursuit beyond the tried and tested, your future talent recipe needs proactive experimentation and adjustment.

Ed Catmull, the person who co-founded Pixar with Steve Jobs, knows a thing or two about creative pursuits which break new ground. He, after all, was the pioneer behind the world's first computer animated motion picture. After putting out tens of blockbuster films, Catmull recently reflected on what made a movie project successful and how the strategy needed to be adjusted during execution.

'Think of building a house. The cheapest way to build it is to draw up the plan for the house and then build to those plans. However, if you've ever been through this process, then you know that as the building takes shape, you say, "What was I thinking? This doesn't work at all." Looking at plans is not the same thing as seeing them realized. Most people who have gone through this say you have to have some extra money because it's going to cost more than you think. And the biggest reason it costs more than you think is that along the way, you realize something you didn't know when you started.'[75]

I find the execution of dynamic capability strategy to be somewhat similar. As we go about optimizing headcount, collaborating with external parties and curating contribution from multiple sources, the execution process and sometimes the strategy itself need to be frequently adjusted. We are, after all, aiming to build breakthrough capability models, rather than blindly copy someone else's best practices.

As an iterative process involving disparate capability sources, any dynamic capability system needs a strong internal governance architecture. As we saw in the 'Your Current Talent Ecosystem' case study in chapter one, this governance is currently broken. HR governs a huge chunk of your talent system—mainly full and part-time employees; Finance manages JVs, mergers and acquisitions; while procurement sources vendors, outsourcing contracts and other types of contractors. Finally, business leaders manage strategic partnerships and consultants, among others. This makes it hard to gain a consolidated view on contribution, the value created, collaboration, cost and most importantly, see how this jigsaw fits together.

The CEO in the role of the Chief Capability Strategist cannot do this by himself or herself.

ENTER: THE TALENT COUNCIL

In our consulting work, one of the solutions which has helped enhance capability governance is the constitution of a Talent

Council to work directly with the CEO on Dynamic Capability strategy.

The Talent Council's primary goal is the integration of governance. Hence, it is best if it is constituted of a small cross-functional group of leaders. I always recommend that the CEO chairs the council and the CHRO (Chief HR Officer) plays the role of the secretary. Other critical members to be included are a very senior finance executive, the head of procurement and a minimum of two senior business executives.

Every council must build its terms of reference, including scope, meeting structure and reporting frequency. From my experience, it should be the council that helps map the current recipe and anchor the overall distributed talent strategy for the business, reporting once every quarter to the organization's executive committee and once a year to the board.

The council may also invite experts as visiting members from time to time, as the agenda dictates. This augmented experience is often in the areas of data protection, cyber security, IT platforms, information management, data analytics and legal.

While the CEO continues to own the talent recipe of the business, the council is his or her arms and legs in the deliberate and purposeful execution of broader talent initiatives. In the final chapter on distributed capability strategy, we will review frameworks and tools which help a Chief Capability Strategist and a talent council to do exactly this.

2. FUTURE-PROOF THE ORGANIZATION'S CAPABILITY RECIPE

The second outcome a Chief Capability Strategist must deliver is an organization built to survive the regular business turbulence which comes from disruptive times. It is their role to imagine the skill shifts and capability footprint required to future-proof the business.

At an industry level, we see two common disruptive forces at play. The first is *technological convergence*, which results in new kinds of products, with the potential to send entire industries into a tailspin, quite like what cellular phones did to fixed-line telephony, or smartphones did to cellular phones, cameras, alarm clocks or watches. Or for that matter, what cloud computing now threatens to do to an entire generation of enterprise hardware and software providers.

The second type of disruptor is best defined by Harvard professor Clayton M. Christensen's model of *disruptive innovation*. These disruptors are innovative solutions which gain industry footholds through radically different customer or cost models, only to creep up the value chain to eventually change an industry's benchmarks. This is what Amazon did to the traditional bookstore, or what Uber is doing to automobile manufacturers and taxi companies across the world.

Both types of disruptors pose serious and rather urgent challenges to traditional industry-leading organizations. And savvy business leaders are responding by disrupting themselves before competitors can, particularly by investing in new ideas which create large economic value for customers or shareholders through the use of new technology. Their goal is clear—stay a step ahead of an industry-wide tsunami.

An example of this can be found in the hospitality industry, where traditional hotel chains are facing competition from apartment sharing sites like Airbnb.

CASE STUDY: AIRBNB

Airbnb was born in 2007 when founders Brian Chesky and Joe Gebbia couldn't afford to pay their rent. Forced to turn their little apartment into shared lodging, they placed three airbeds on the floor and offered them to potential renters using a simple website.

Little did they realize that this was the start of a revolution which would, in time, threaten the world's biggest hotel chains. Within a decade of its formal launch in 2008, the company has helped sixty million guests find temporary accommodation, and offered over two million rooms in 34,000 cities.

Airbnb is much more than a company which allows us to rent out our spare rooms to strangers. It is a cult brand with young travellers. And it is this fact more than anything else that is giving most traditional hoteliers sleepless nights. Airbnb's core demographic is the millennial traveller. As more millennials come of age and travel, they seem to share an intuitive affinity for the informality and diversity of the sharing economy. Contrast this with the stuffy and bland standardized rooms offered by most large hotel brands, targeting the legions of jaded middle-aged business travellers.

This makes Airbnb a perfect example of disruptive innovation in the hotel business. It targeted a previously neglected end of the market—the young and price-conscious traveller, offering them a differentiated experience. This has forced the bigger hotel chains to respond with their own millennial-friendly brand offerings.

Marriott recently launched its Moxy range of hotels with an eye on the specific needs of young travellers. Located in city centres near bars and other nightlife, Moxy hotels are small, reasonably priced and built around communal spaces like living rooms and game rooms, where travellers can mingle and make friends. Similarly, in early 2016, Hilton launched its millennial brand called Tru by Hilton. According to the hotel chain, 'The brand will appeal to a broad range of travellers who span generations but think alike; they are united by a millennial mindset—a youthful energy, a zest for life and a desire for human connection.' Each Tru offers a large open space called 'The Hive', encouraging guests to hang out together, as well as social media walls displaying real-time content.

If there is one lesson in this case study, it is that businesses cannot be insular and inward-looking any more. Disruptors can come from anywhere and increasingly they come from outside the industry itself, making them hard to spot until it is too late.

Moreover, they all don't need to be new ideas like Airbnb. This is also an age of technological convergence, where traditional technologies can get turbocharged by new digital capability.

BUILDING VUCA READY ORGANIZATIONS

Disruptive times call for VUCA savvy leaders. A nifty acronym coined by the US military to describe the changing nature of armed conflict after the fall of the Soviet Union, VUCA stood for the four concurrent geopolitical pressures of volatility, uncertainty, complexity and ambiguity that the US armed forces would have to face in an age where the enemy was less defined. Over the last twenty-five years, this acronym has travelled from military parlance to the business lexicon. It shouldn't surprise us then to learn that in Zulu, the ancient language of Southern Africa, the word 'vuca', when translated, means 'wake up'!

I see many business leaders struggling in a VUCA world and starting to question if, in an age of frequent shifts, long-term strategic planning makes sense anymore. 'If the future is undefined, do we need a strategy at all?' some ask.

Yes, we do! Because both inaction and delayed reaction are terrible business choices for leaders. Hence, the need to have nimbler and more VUCA-savvy leadership. For one, the four independent challenges of volatility, uncertainty, complexity and ambiguity do not apply to every business. Some face one more than the others, while others, particularly those in the midst of systemic change, will have to contend with all four VUCA challenges concurrently.

The first step for any leader is to understand what these four actualities mean to the art and craft of business management. It is only after thoroughly understanding them that we can start considering a strategic response. Fig. 8.1 gives a framework that I use to coach leaders on VUCA realities in business.

DECONSTRUCTING VUCA SITUATIONS IN BUSINESS

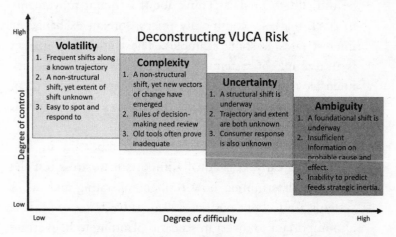

Fig. 8.1: VUCA Realities in Business

As you can see in this illustration, the four circumstances that constitute VUCA are not equal. They are materially different in both the *degree of difficulty* they individually pose to a business and the *degree of control* this business has on each situation. Some businesses may face more complexity and less volatility, while others may be dealing with higher levels of uncertainty or ambiguity.

A framework such as this helps us understand the symptoms better. It also helps us disaggregate what could look like a debilitating challenge into well-defined individual components, which can then be addressed both individually and collectively. This makes both sensing and responding to VUCA situations an essential part of 21st-century leadership competence. Let's understand each variable in increasing degree of difficulty:

1. *Volatility*: It is the easiest circumstance to diagnose. It denotes frequent shifts along a known trajectory, making volatility easier to spot and hence react to. Volatility poses significant challenges, as often the direction and extent of this shift can be difficult to predict. Think about frequent movements in stock markets, commodity prices, foreign exchange or interest rates as some examples. The commodity market is an example of systemic volatility. The capital and time-intensive nature of resource-driven businesses makes them ripe for demand-and-supply imbalances and resultant boom-and-bust cycles.

   When dealing with volatility, it is important to spot the triggers early. It is equally important to stress test the business, determining how resilient operating and talent systems are to both positive and negative trajectories. It is also important to invest in scenario planning to help create both an offensive and defensive playbook. This approach can help save precious time when change happens.

2. *Complexity*: It sits a step above volatility in difficulty, and is equally a governance dilemma. The word comes from

complexus in Latin which, in turn, has two parts—'plexus' which means 'intertwined' and 'cum' which is a Latin prefix for 'with'.

Hence, complexity emerges from an increase in interwoven variables which merit both increased focus and consideration. Decisionmaking becomes tougher, as new decision variables get added. As a non-structural shift, complexity is easy to spot and adapt to. In doing so, we must recognize that the inertia of past successes can be our greatest enemy. As the circumstances of business become more complex, we must abandon outdated methods and decision models in favour of new ones.

Responsible decentralization is one possible solution to this dilemma. Other approaches include simplification and prioritization of organizational processes, as well as greater sharing of critical information, thereby enhancing informed decisionmaking.

As someone who does much work in the African continent, I see the complexity of providing urgent and critical health care in some of the world's poorest nations as one such example. The problem's multifaceted nature, in the form of chronic illiteracy, poor hygiene, inadequate information and a severe shortfall in medicine and equipment, is often amplified by religious and cultural dogma which is taking years to break down. This makes the HIV and Ebola epidemics in Africa pertinent examples of systemic complexity, where multiple variables are at play.

3. *Uncertainty*: It is much more difficult to contend with uncertainty than both business volatility and complexity. This is because uncertainty may in itself be a consequence of larger socio-economic or geopolitical shifts.

Often, uncertainty emerges when an industry is in transition, driven not just by new ways of working but entirely new products, new customers or revenue models. These present both uncontrollable challenges and wide-ranging opportunities for emerging market-makers.

Navigating uncertainty requires new ideas and investments which generate new understanding. Strengthening research and investing in insight are some of the best strategies in times of uncertainty. It will also serve us well to gear up for quick pivots as the market changes. Several industries find themselves in this zone of uncertainty today. The publishing business is an example, where the onslaught of free content on the internet has resulted in the slow and painful unwinding of a 200-year-old literary and publishing rubric.

4. *Ambiguity*: It is probably the hardest of all four circumstances. In ambiguous times, even the simplest answers are in doubt. This perpetuates an intellectual gridlock, as both cause and effect are unclear. Thus, ambiguity poses the greatest leadership challenge and often requires a slice of luck for the pieces of the jigsaw to fall in place.

Still, there are several strategies that leaders have at their disposal. A popular one is to hedge against change through diversification of products and customers. Ambiguity is also a great time to invest in broad alliances which enhance 'sense-making' at an industry-wide level. In ambiguous times, no singular business has all the answers, hence collaborating beyond our normal comfort zones may lead to fresh insights and new approaches.

I often think of the climate debate and the role traditional energy companies play in it, as an example. We can no longer wish away the impact fossil fuels have on climate change and can't deny their contribution to greenhouse effects. Moreover, while climate change threatens the current industry's existence in the long term, it also presents an opportunity for collective action and reinvention of the energy business. This is exactly what we see happening, with the largest energy companies in Europe collectively choosing to collaborate rather than compete with regulators in solving climate change.

The illustration in fig. 8.2 captures some of the ideas we discussed above and presents a map of strategic actions executives can take in VUCA times.

A STRATEGIC PLAYBOOK FOR VUCA

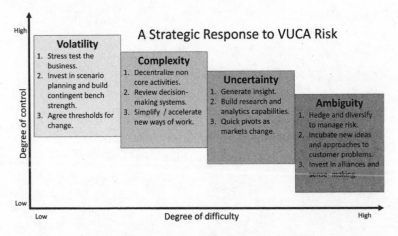

Fig. 8.2: VUCA: Possible Strategic Actions

Capability systems are very susceptible to VUCA shifts. Because of their rather long-term nature, an organization's talent system can frequently be out of sync with fast-paced shifts in business circumstances. The best example can be found in the case study on 'Oil Volatility and the True Cost of Functional Delivery' that we saw in chapter four.

In the past, organizations have responded to market shifts by bingeing on or purging headcount which, as we have seen, can be devastating for morale and incredibly costly as a strategy. It is critical that Chief Capability Officers and the Talent Council be strong at sensing VUCA risk and equally adept at building a talent recipe which is flexible and responsive in nature.

9

BUILDING THE FUTURE-
READY ORGANIZATION
Cultivating Capability

I hire people brighter than me and I get out of their way.

—Lee Iacocca

The previous chapter covered the leadership needed in Future-
Ready Organizations and the governance needs of dynamic
capability systems.

This chapter (and the next one) take the discussion one level
deeper, with a clear goal to explore the two distinct responsibilities
of a Dynamic Capability Manager. This chapter deals with the
first responsibility, which I call the manager's goal to *cultivate
capability*, and covers new-age techniques to find the best talent
within a distributed talent system. Before going forward, let's first
understand why current strategies to find talent are falling woefully
short.

179

A DISHONEST DANCE

Claudio Fernandez-Araoz is a bestselling author and global expert on hiring at Egon Zehnder, one of the world's largest executive search firms. A specialist in finding talent, Fernandez-Araoz has interviewed over 20,000 candidates in over thirty years in the search business. So I chuckled a little when, in a recent news article, this industry veteran called the typical interview 'a conversation between two liars'.[76]

Fernandez-Araoz is right. And he isn't the only one saying so. A study conducted at the University of Massachusetts found that 81 per cent of applicants lied during job interviews. A typical fifteen-minute interview, the research team found, contained an average of 2.19 lies.[77] In theory, this shouldn't be a problem, because seasoned interviewers can easily spot these lies. Right?

Well, think again. As a co-author of the study, Ron Friedman wrote in a subsequent book: 'The unfortunate truth is this: we're rarely effective in picking out dishonesty. We are only slightly better at determining if someone has lied to our face than we are at predicting whether a flipped coin will land on its head. Seasoned interviewers are no better than novices. They are, however, significantly different in one respect—although they are just as bad as everyone else at recognizing deception, they feel significantly more confident in their conclusions.'[78]

It isn't just dishonesty that makes interviews a poor filter. Research has found that interviewers often fall victim to the two other common tactics of conscious deception. The first is *ingratiation*. Coined by social psychologist Edward E. Jones, ingratiation describes the common practice of using false praise for the organization or flattery for the interviewer to appear more genial and likeable. The second tactic is *impression management* (IM), which describes how individuals can deceptively influence the impressions others have of them in social interactions. Together, both ingratiation and IM significantly distort applicant performance. It could be argued that IM plays a regular role in daily social interactions too, and hence is something which gets informally discounted.

However, in interview situations, research has found that IM can get dangerously amplified or exaggerated.[79] IM behaviour can range from the infantile—like following absurd and silly fashions to appear cool or confident (think of all the multicoloured socks being worn under staid suits), to the outright dangerous— like failing to disclose a previous firing or an unresolved sexual harassment complaint at a previous employment.

While the applicant is under greater scrutiny, often the deception can come from the opposite side of the table too. Interviewers use similar techniques to woo desired skills or hide critical flaws in company culture or performance.

And herein lies the problem. Because interviews are ubiquitous, we all use them to hire talent. Yet, they are probably among the worst possible tools for the initial screening of candidates. The pressure to perform forces both parties to dress up in more ways than one. This is ironic because a significant relationship cannot be built on anything but honesty and truth.

THE MENTAL HIJACK

Probably the biggest factor in the ineffectiveness of interviews as a filter for top skills is the vast role predispositions and biases play in candidate selection. Our brains subconsciously process so much information in the first few minutes of meeting a new person that it becomes virtually impossible not to be influenced by good looks, deep or considered speech, height, clothes or even hairstyles, among other things.

Taken together, these predispositions, biases and the nebulous notion of culture fit—which 43 per cent of managers[80] cite as the single-most important factor in the hiring decision—are the main reason many deserving candidates don't get hired. Researchers in psychology call this 'norm activation' which is an almost subconscious mobilization of cognitive reasoning structures based on an interviewer's assumption of who is 'an ideal candidate'. This assumption, in turn, triggers an emotional response to what a candidate says or does, something social cognition researchers Barrick, Shaffer and DeGrassi call 'affective evaluation', what we commonly know as the 'halo effect'.

If you couple this with Herbert Simon's concept of 'satisficing' which we reviewed in chapter seven, human beings left to industrial-era selection tools like CVs and interviews are probably the poorest decision-makers on future potential. Also, Simon's insight proves why Friedman's proposition that 'experienced recruiters are just as poor as inexperienced ones' rings true. I feel we need a lot more than conversational and intuitive filters, because the people who perform well in interviews are often different from those who perform on the job.

VIDEO SCREENING ISN'T A TECHNOLOGICAL ENHANCEMENT

I often worry that the growing popularity of video screening tools could be making this problem worse. These systems, with a few variations, generally ask candidates to record and submit canned answers to preset questions via offline video.

As a tool, video screening does drive efficiency on the surface, as it significantly cuts out commutes and venues and scheduling conflicts, for what is effectively a first-level screen. It also gives the interviewer greater flexibility—to view candidate videos at any time, keep record or rewind and review answers.

However, the question this raises is: does the instant, static and unidirectional nature of this emerging technology also enhance the impact of predispositions and bias? If so, then this is the wrong use of technology, because it exacerbates the significant risk already inherent within other selection methodologies in common use today.

AVOIDING THE 'SATISFICING' TRAP

A recruiter falling victim of norm activation or applicant deception is only a minor reason for poor selection performance. The major reason for poor selection, it turns out, is because the interview is woefully inadequate as an early filter. Like a sculptor taking a sledgehammer to a block of fine marble, the interview is a tool which doesn't fit the purpose for which it is used.

The most shocking selection errors (rejecting the right or selecting the wrong) often occur during the first rounds, when time available per candidate is the least. After all, a screening interview is rarely about finding the right candidate. It is often about rejecting the outlier. This is also where the battle is often lost because, in the absence of any deep understanding of a candidate's true capability, our preferences and prejudices drive the decision. Research has shown that inconsequential criteria like a person's name,[81] height, dress sense or their leisure activities have significantly skewed selection decisions.

Hiring poor quality, especially in balance-sheet talent positions, is one of the most significant risks in your dynamic capability system. As this is, by definition, your least flexible pool of individuals, your selection process must ensure the right capability is filtered properly, irrespective of what it may look like.

While poor as an initial filter, the interview does still work well as a tool for final selection, because at this point, there should be a mountain of evidence on the candidate's competence. This downgrades our gut, and its innate predisposition for satisficed decisions, to less consequential criteria.

Herbert Simon saw technology and AI as a means, go beyond human cognitive limits, process more information faster and make better decisions. Fortunately, even without AI, today, managers have access to several powerful new channels and tools which supplement human decision-making. However, for this to work, we must support interviews with more accurate tools to help us select the right people.

TEN PRACTICAL IDEAS TO CULTIVATE DYNAMIC CAPABILITY

1. *Auditions and Performance Challenges*

Selecting talent is an imperfect science. That is because in the end, all decisions are still being made by human beings. The biggest problem is that often our first-round screening of candidates is so poor, a job lottery might perform better than us.

CASE STUDY: THE BLIND AUDITION

Through most of the early 1900s, the pinnacle of any classical musician's ambitions was a regular spot in a top-rated symphony orchestra. And yet, while many women played exceptionally well in the junior ranks, in almost all the world's top orchestras, most musicians were male. In fact, before the 1970s, 95 per cent of the top five orchestras in the US were male. The sexism in music ran so deep that two of the most respected conductors of the last century were rumoured to deeply believe that men play better than women at the highest level.

But everything changed when the New York Philharmonic was sued for racial bias by two black musicians in 1969. At that time, the Philharmonic had one black musician out of 106 in the orchestra.

As a direct consequence, in the 1970s and 1980s, many top orchestras started experimenting with blind auditions to avoid similar legal challenges. First tested at the Boston Philharmonic years earlier in 1952, blind auditions required musicians to play from behind a curtain or screen, so that music directors and other members of the jury could not see them. Curiously, initial tests on gender neutral hiring proved to be a failure because jury members could discern the distinct sound of shoes worn by a man or woman on the wooden stage. The ratios didn't improve at all.

But once this was addressed by laying down a carpet and asking candidates to remove their shoes when they came on stage to play, the blind audition changed classical music for ever.

As Curt Rice, a professor at the University of Tromsø, explains, 'Even when the screen is only used for the preliminary round, it has a powerful impact, researchers have determined that this step alone makes it 50% more likely that a woman will advance to the finals. And the screen has also been demonstrated to be the source of a surge in the number of women being offered positions.'[82]

It isn't surprising that since the early 1980s, around half the musicians hired at the New York Philharmonic and one in three at Boston have been women.

One of the best ways to avoid recruiter bias and other forms of passive discrimination is to ensure that a 'competence screen' exists before the recruiter's gut can take over. Fortunately today, we have a number of technology-enabled blind audition programmes which help you do just that.

An example is GapJumpers, who have successfully taken the concept of blind auditions from the symphony stages and reality music shows like 'The Voice' and used it to build a powerful early selection tool for hiring managers. Their job search engine, like most, allows a hiring manager to advertise jobs along with the key skills they need. But there is more. Each job post also includes online skill or scenario-based tests, called the 'performance audition challenge'. These challenges are designed to test current skills as opposed to past experiences. For example, when the *Guardian* newspaper in the UK was looking for an account manager for media solutions, the associated challenge asked candidates to research current issues to design a media plan focused on small businesses in UK. Another post for an Art Director in Beirut asked candidates for illustrations which could be used to sell Volvo cars in the UAE.

Once a challenge is closed, hiring managers just see candidate responses and scores, without any biographical data, not even a name. Only after the best have been selected, GapJumper, makes the complete resume available.

Another approach to early competent testing could be what firms like Automattic—the open-source powerhouse behind Wordpress.com—use. They have short-term contracts, called 'try-outs' as a way to audition and pick the right talent. As Automattic's CEO Matt Mullenweg wrote in a recent commentary, 'The most significant shift we've made is requiring every final candidate to work with us for three to eight weeks on a contract basis. Candidates do real tasks alongside the people they would actually be working with if they had the job. They can work at night or on weekends, so they don't have to leave their current jobs; most spend 10 to 20 hours a week working with Automattic, although that's flexible.'

Auttomattic doesn't expect free work during the try-out. Mullenweg says, 'To keep it simple, we decided to pay a standard $25 an hour, whether the candidate was hoping to be an engineer or the chief financial officer.'[83]

2. *The Peer-to-Peer Micro Challenge*

Extreme interviews were popularized by Steve Jobs and the folks at Google. Designed to get a candidate rattled and check how they respond to unfamiliar scenarios and stress, the extreme interview is a ploy to crack open the prepared masquerade most candidates put on for interviews and gain a glimpse at who the person behind the mask really is.

Extreme interviewing can be a mixed bag. While helpful in mining unscripted answers and avoiding ingratiation, it still doesn't predict efficacy. After all, personality isn't performance and often, a candidate's performance in an interview is not a good proxy for performance on the job. There is one company, though, that builds extreme interview situations around its innate culture and work practices.

CASE STUDY: MENLO INNOVATIONS

Richard Sheridan is the author of the 2013 book *Joy, Inc.: How We Built a Workplace People Love*. Sheridan is also a co-founder of Menlo Innovations, a software development company with no reporting lines, no job titles and no one works alone—literally. Almost all work at Menlo is done in pairs. Two people share a single computer, keyboard and mouse and stay together for a week. As Sheridan describes it, 'Pairing is the most powerful managerial tool ever discovered. It makes so many things change and change rapidly. The fact that we assign the pairs and switch them every five days, and sometimes sooner, this creates a human energy that is unstoppable.'[84]

Working in pairs and switching projects weekly are two distinct parts of Menlo culture. And their extreme interview mimics exactly this. There are no questions. Not even a preamble. All candidates are paired up and assigned micro-challenges to work on, with a Menlo staff member observing them. After twenty minutes, they are reassigned to another team. Those who perform in the pair-challenges assigned to them then spend an entire day working with Menlo staff. The message to candidates is clear—Menlo is looking for collaborators, as opposed to industry superstars.

What's critical to note is that through both rounds, it is fellow Menlonians who decide whom to call back. If an individual's happiness and success at work depends on the quality of peers who surround them, peer-hiring is probably the approach of choice.

3. Talent-Spotting

The chances of the stars aligning to deliver us a perfect candidate, exactly when we are hiring, are abysmally low. Fortunately, there are quite a few good people out there, who cross our path throughout the year, and could be a valuable addition to internal talent. Throughout my career, the best hires I made were mostly off-cycle talent selections—people I had worked with in contingent roles or were employed by other companies when our paths crossed.

In their roles as constant cultivators of capability, Dynamic Capability Managers must tune their talent-spotting radars to work continuously. And once you cross paths with exceptional people who could add exponential value as internal talent, I would encourage you to visibly communicate this to them. Even if a role isn't available or the individual isn't looking to move just yet. This communication often proves seductive in retrospect, because it is authentic and motivated by genuine confidence in the ability of the other person. Here's an example of how one company has institutionalized this practice:

CASE STUDY: 'YOU'RE AMAZING' CARDS

With over 10,000 employees in its fast-growing retail store network, Apple gives its recruiters a bunch of cards (fig. 9.1) to hand out whenever they come across a retail individual anywhere who delivered great service. The simple cards read, 'You're amazing. We should talk.' And when you flip them over, they read, 'Your customer service just now was exceptional. I work for the Apple Store, and you're exactly the kind of person we'd like to talk to. If you're happy where you are, I'd never ask you to leave. But if you're thinking about a change, give me a call. This could be the start of something great.'

Fig. 9.1: Card from Apple

Apple is showing us that the identification of great talent is an ongoing process as opposed to a sporadic one.

4. *Mid and Late-Career Internships*

Talent economics data shows that somewhere between twenty and thirty-two million white-collar employees have been displaced since the global financial crisis in 2008. In addition, some estimates show that as many as 37 per cent of qualified women experience some form of a mid-career break. Now add to this the many millions of middle-aged talent stuck in dead-end jobs and looking for career reboots. These are three potent sources for a structured programme of mid and late-career internships. These internships, which normally last between three and six months, are probably the best entry opportunities for mid-career talent, as they allow both parties to test the waters before deciding on a specific role for an experienced hire. Some companies like Goldman Sachs and Sara Lee have been using them for years; other have only just started.

A rise in life expectancy, improved healthcare and the gradual breakdown of retirement thresholds are three of the many reasons making the prospect of mid-career internships quite interesting. Coupled with flexible work packages, they could be great sources of mature talent with strong transferable skills. What we know now is that after Robert De Niro hit a collective nerve by starring as a 70-year-old late-career intern in the 2015 hit film *The Intern*, he was just highlighting an active trend. Companies like PricewaterhouseCoopers have recently started older intern programs, and in 2015, Barclays kicked off a year-long 'Bolder Apprenticeships' for candidates below 65.[85]

5. *Proxies like Social Reputation*

An exciting, if relatively recent, channel to identify top talent is through their social reputation. Social collaboration websites are often ideal places to find great internal talent. The mega knowledge-sharing community of close to seven million programmers on

Stack Overflow represents what is probably the best test-case for social reputational hiring. While Stack Overflow is mainly for programmers, its sister site Stack Exchange has Q&A communities on thousands of other topics ranging from quantum physics to gardening. Both are monster-sized, self-moderating peer-to-peer question-and-answer sites.

Because Stack does such a great job of quantifying reputation, with community members constantly upvoting or downvoting every interaction based on how useful, innovative or responsive it is, stack reputation has become a solid indicator of expertise, helpfulness and responsiveness. A senior development director I know well uses stack overflow as well as some other open-source collaboration sites like Open Hub and GitHub as the primary source for sourcing his tech talent.

Outside of technology, it is quite the same with other social sites liked LinkedIn or Twitter. People who have built social capital from the bottom-up have invariably done so by communicating and collaborating.

This is an incredibly valuable future skill given the enormous complexity of the digital age. We live in times when no one person can possibly have all the answers. Talent which is well connected, responsible and responsive has a better chance of reaching out and getting help when they need it while helping others with what they know. A good reputation and good followership could also validate topical expertise in fast-moving times. Reading through the individual's posts and answers could give you a deeper sense of their voice, communication style, level of patience and even empathy.

There is one caveat, though. I am wary of hiring superstar networkers who gain social reputation by spending half their life on social media. For me, a good, positive and diverse social presence scores over those with the highest social scores or followers.

6. *Gaming and Hackathons*

Gaming is a great way to connect with millennial talent. For example, using gamification techniques, Domino's offers the Pizza Mogul game in Australia to build brand connection and affinity, particularly among high-school kids. On the other end of the spectrum, looking for potential spies and code-crackers in 2011, British intelligence agency GCHQ (Government Communications Headquarters) used an online code game at http://www.canyoucrackit.co.uk/ to reach candidates well beyond their regular recruitment channels. The legacy of the GCHQ code game goes back to the search for code-breakers during the Second World War.

CASE STUDY: BLETCHLEY PARK

Located in the leafy suburb of Buckinghamshire, fifty miles northwest of London, one finds Bletchley Park, the exact spot where many believe the Second World War was won. It was here that British code-breakers from the British Government Code and Cypher School (GC&CS), led by mathematician Alan Turing, eventually deciphered the reportedly unbreakable Enigma code used by the German army. Historians point to this as the critical pivot in the war, leading to several Allied victories including the decisive Battle of the Atlantic.

The Bletchley Park pack of code-breakers once used a crossword puzzle placed in the *Daily Telegraph* newspaper to secretly recruit talent. Crossword puzzles, it turns out, follow similar principles as code setting. Solving them, hence, require similar skills too, like logical and lateral thinking as well as creative approaches to problem-solving. The word 'enigma' after all, is the Greek word for puzzle.

James Grime, an expert on Alan Turing, concurs, 'It was problem solvers they needed; unconventional thinkers to solve the problem.'[86] The *Daily Telegraph* crossword puzzle they placed innocuously on 13 January 1942 asked those who solved it under twelve minutes to call in.

Games can be great ways to gain a glimpse at creative skills. Fig 9.2 has the original crossword if you would like a crack at it:

Source: The Telegraph UK Multimedia Archives[87]
Fig. 9.2: *The Telegraph* Crossword

The modern hackathon hiring event has the same DNA of creative problem-solving. Hackathons are increasingly being used as hiring tools from Ivy League campuses to business parks in Hyderabad or Hanoi. Usually immersive events of forty-eight hours or less, the hackathon is an opportunity to flesh out ideas and prototype solutions on a given theme. The best ideators, the strongest lateral thinkers and the dogged problem solvers thrive in hackathon environments, and it is for this reason that they are the preferred hiring platform for start-ups looking to scale after a funding round. Once considered purely the domain of technology buffs, we find that more non-tech companies are experimenting with them too. This is because the hackathon is a great way to access the truly innovative talent out there. Even financial services firms like DBS bank now use hackathons extensively.

7. Case Study Contests for Campus Hiring

Another tool is the case study contest. Think of it as a performance challenge or audition for inexperienced hires. Hence, it is becoming a popular tool for campus hiring at levels below the MBA class (where case-based hiring has been employed since the late 1970s). By using cases built on real-life situations within the company, the students also gain valuable insight into company strategy, culture, products and practices.

More recently, I have seen case studies become a part of the company's global hiring strategy, rather than just a tool. This is a smart choice because it also gives you a common yardstick to help identify the best sources of talent on a relative basis. For example, seeking to adapt to the changing engagement needs of millennial engineers and to increase interaction between the organization and its potential graduate hires, Munich headquartered international electronics firm Rohde & Schwarz successfully used a global case study competition as a key component of their campus hiring program. In 2015, 350 students across twenty campus events in North America, Europe and Asia spent an entire day with the company's engineers and HR team, solving case study problems placed in front of them. Fifty-four winners of these preliminary rounds then flew to Germany for a two-day final competition. The net result was twenty-one interns and twelve graduate hires for the company.

8. *Your Alumni*

With the emotion and stigma associated with resignations fading, your own alumni become a potent source of talent, be it through a formal network or alumni association (think McKinsey, Credit Suisse, Facebook or Netflix) or through informal means.

We all have strong personal and professional social networks, with a lot of ex-colleagues (now friends) on them. This makes it incredibly easy to mine and connect with high-performing talent which may have moved on but could come back for the right offer. And returning to an ex-employer is a very popular strategy for millennial talent. As the number of these digital natives progressively grow as a percentage of the workforce, so will alumni programs.

9. *Contractors and Outsourced Talent*

With high-quality freelance talent available, companies are warming up to transient project opportunities as a great means to select external talent.

Start-ups, in particular, rely heavily on the 'human cloud' of freelance workers to find future internal talent. It is easy to find entrepreneurial freelancers this way, which suits start-ups perfectly, as they often prioritize entrepreneurial thinking along with creative problem-solving and flexibility as the top three traits they look for in early stage employees. Given rapidly evolving dynamic capability structures, both your external and network talent could prove a happy hunting ground for internal talent. You have a chance to work with this talent and test technical, customer and collaboration skills before offering them something more permanent. If top freelance talent enjoys working for you, they might just agree.

Contingent talent can be one of the best sources of technical and managerial talent too. For example, starting 2004, in the early and high growth phase of the global outsourcing industry, I spent three years stewarding the Asian talent agenda at one of the world's largest IT and offshore companies. In one vertical, we employed thousands of software engineers to troubleshoot enterprise applications for a Fortune 100 software company's customers. We would spend millions on hiring, training and certifying this talent, who within a couple of years of tricky troubleshooting calls would end up mastering all the finer nuances of the software. With little left to learn, many would soon leave for more promising programming careers.

Looking to resolve this haemorrhage, as an experiment, we requested the client organization to come over once a year and interview some of the most experienced support engineers for internal software development and testing roles. The brightest got picked immediately. This ended up creating a huge win-win situation for both our client and for us as their outsourced partner. They saw us as a fertile training ground for highly competent future hires and we could access and retain even better talent due to the career path we now provided.

A mature contingent strategy gives you access to a unique, diverse, vibrant and entrepreneurial talent pool which often flies below the radar of your regular recruiters and search consultants.

10. *Aquihiring*
The practice of acquiring a company primarily for its employees, rather than its technology, brand, customers or revenue streams, has been rising in popularity over the last decade. The trend hit an early peak in the years just after the global financial crisis, where several early ventures starved for cash looked at being acquired as a lifeline, and an opportunity to still work together—what is popularly known as a 'soft landing' in the start-up business.

What followed through 2010 and 2011 was a large number of fast-growing mega-brands, like Zynga, Google, Facebook, Twitter and LinkedIn, snapped up tens of subscale start-ups for eye-popping sums. In an industry strapped for high-quality talent, these acquisitions were quick capability 'booster shots'. However, many ended up as failures, with teams disintegrating within months after the acquisition.

Unless the acquired talent is integrated carefully into the new organization, given meaningful projects to work on and kept together, this strategy tends to fail. Often, if the acquirer has no interest in the past ideas, technology and products, many of the acquired founders and key talent, with new millions in the pocket, just bide their time through earn-out periods and promptly quit to start new ventures. In other instances, many acquihires have been done purely for engineering talent, with the founders not being offered jobs. In these cases, many engineers leave and go back to work for those founders on new ventures they may have started.

All these episodes have taught acquiring companies valuable lessons, and though it is used more judiciously now, acquihire is still a powerful source of strategic talent. And some do it better than others. Facebook, for one, has scored big with its acquisitions, from WhatsApp to Instagram and tens of others. In part, because they recognize the value of people they are acquiring. As Mark Zuckerberg once told a Y Combinator forum, 'Facebook has not once bought a company for the company itself. We buy companies to get excellent people.'[88]

10

BUILDING THE FUTURE-READY ORGANIZATION
Curating Contribution

If you can hire people whose passion intersects with the job, they won't require any supervision at all. They will manage themselves better than anyone could ever manage them. Their fire comes from within, not from without. Their motivation is internal, not external.

—*Stephen Covey*

Beyond finding the best capability, getting a distributed talent system to work together is what creates real value in the here-and-now. And the managers who achieve this look nothing like their industrial-era ancestors. The industrial economy put a premium on the repetitive delivery of process-driven factory work. This is what delivered quality products consistently. The knowledge economy is quite different in that it puts a premium on cognitive decision-making, collaborative problem-solving and creative thinking. This is what delivers innovation.

Watching the best scrum masters in action, there is one thing that strikes me more than anything. They focus on issues rather than the individual—a simple pivot that helps us reframe the role of a traditional supervisor.

There are four main principles Dynamic Capability Managers must imbue to unlock value from 21st-century talent.

1. TALENT SEEKS A FAIR EXCHANGE OF VALUE

New-age talent isn't beholden to a single job or even to work for that matter like previous generations were. Most see the time they invest at work as a means to an end. This makes it critically important for managers to understand what constitutes this 'end'.

Money is a big part of it, but rarely is it all of it. Increasingly, evidence shows us that the power of money as a motivator in aggregate is grossly overstated. It is true that people value money a lot more when they are unable to meet basic needs. But once people are paid a fair wage, the incremental value of money as a motivator depreciates rather quickly.

The million-dollar question then is—What is a fair wage? Is it what the market decides to pay a fast food employee versus a hedge fund manager? Is it the accepted hourly wage in Switzerland or Somalia? Or is it purely the number on the contract signed between the two parties?

Economically speaking, it could be all of these. Then why is it that two individuals doing the same work for the same pay in the same location rarely share the same level of wage satisfaction?

Primarily, because each individual's orientation to money is different, as is their need for it. A fair wage, therefore, is as much about perceptions and relative value as it is about numbers. In the laboratory of global business, this effect has been proven multiple times since 1990, mainly by the millions of jobs outsourced internationally for wage arbitrage reasons. If two people of comparable skills have a different perception of value in return, the job itself tends to flow to the person willing to do it for less.

This book, however, isn't about global trade or outsourcing. It is about 21st-century talent, that is, talented individuals looking to monetize skills and ability, by creating economic value for others. Hence, acknowledging the relative and emotive nature of 'worth', a fair wage is nothing but an economic and emotional threshold at which an individual no longer worries about immediate financial security. It is the point at which the focus shifts from the pay to the work itself.

BEYOND MONEY

This is precisely why industries which traditionally overwork money as a motivator are in deep trouble. It is also why banks are no longer the preferred employer on college campuses or why makers of tobacco products are struggling to schedule interviews in spite of offering better-than-market compensation.

Once an offer is at or above a mental threshold, talent today is much more discerning. They seek jobs which create social value while allowing their own skills to develop. To be more specific, once money as a motive has fully played out, there is another motive which proves critically important to 21st-century talent.

CREATIVE FREEDOM

In a 2013 study, the *Economist* found clear evidence of an inverse correlation between productivity and hours spent at work.[89] In other words, the longer people worked the less productive they were. Perhaps more encouragingly, they found that within the OECD countries (a group of thirty-four relatively developed free-market economies) working hours had steadily declined over the last twenty years. The Japanese, Koreans, Portuguese, French and Germans are working significantly fewer hours today than they were in 1990. This is an encouraging sign but by no means a definitive indicator. Because since 1990, the very nature of industry has changed with the birth and explosive growth of the knowledge economy.

And this makes things much more complicated. While it is easy to observe and track productivity in traditional businesses like manufacturing or services, it is considerably more challenging to ascertain productivity in knowledge work. Cognitive work, by definition, is difficult to quantify and supervise in the short term. Managers hence have resorted to surrogate measures to judge an individual's performance: like time spent at work, or time spent in front of a computer screen, or arriving early and staying late. These measures, while easily observable, are poor proxies for productivity in the world of knowledge work and has only led to more distrust of managers.

It has taken management sciences an incredibly long time to wake up to the fact that for knowledge workers, cognitive engagement is vastly more important than physical presence. And this makes connecting with the ideas hidden within our talent very important, because ideas do what tedious supervision cannot— they raise initiative.

In my first book *Talent Economics*, I described what a 'flow organization' looks like. This is an organization where everyone has space, time and support to sharpen their axe. The first step to generating flow is through an atmosphere where employees feel comfortable sharing their ideas and taking risks to try new things. This takes courage. It also takes a genuine invitation, and we must now consciously teach managers to coach and champion employee genius, rather than get in the way of flow. At an organizational level, the more examples you showcase, the greater flow you generate. The best talent values this, with many reporting creative freedom on par with compensation as a career driver.

A famous example is Google. In their 2004 IPO note, Larry Page and Sergie Brin wrote, 'We encourage our employees, in addition to their regular projects, to spend 20% of their time working on what they think will most benefit Google. This empowers them to be more creative and innovative. Many of our significant advances have happened in this manner.'[90] Now well known simply as '20% time' the only condition is that the ideas must relate in some way to Google's work. To say that this policy of giving people time off to work on their own ideas has paid off is an understatement. This opportunity to incubate ideas in private has led to iconic products like AdSense, Gmail and the Chromebook.[91]

I came across another delightful example a few years ago. Sitting in a cinema hall with my daughter, waiting for the movie *Inside Out* to begin, the screen suddenly lit up with the image of a volcano in the midst of the sea and a single word 'LAVA'. What followed was an enjoyable five-minute song set to the ukulele. My daughter was mesmerized and most parents like me quite puzzled. I checked the ticket stub. Had we wandered into the wrong hall? A couple of lines later, everyone around me, young and old alike, were totally immersed in the song about a lonely volcano pining for a mate. So much so that the audience applauded at the end of this short music video, if one could call it that. And then the real movie began. I remember thinking, 'That was a masterstroke.' The makers of the film had just 'marinated' the audience into the right emotional state before the main movie began.

Walking home later, I asked my 8-year-old what she loved most about the film we had just watched. The answer was, 'I Lava You.'

Ed Catmull, the 70-year-old President of Pixar Animation Studios, now owned by Disney, which made both *Inside Out* and *I Lava You*, puts it perfectly, 'We put short films at the beginning of our movies. Why? Nobody is going to go to a movie because of the shorts, and neither the theatre owners nor Disney gets any more money because of them.

So why do the shorts? Well, we are sending some signals. It is a signal to the audience that we're giving them more than they're paying for, a signal to the artistic community that Pixar and Disney are encouraging broader artistic expression, and a signal to our employees that we're doing something for which we don't get any money. While they all know that we have to make money and want us to, they also want a signal that we are not so driven by money that it trumps everything else.'[92]

TIME IS TRUST

More organizations are following suit, and some even encourage employees to use paid time to work on ideas that are not related to work. For example, Viget, a well-known digital agency, encourages its staff to use gaps between client projects to work on their own ideas. They even have a name and website for it—PointlessCorp.com.

Pointless Corp has created a bunch of tools, games and apps over the years that have nothing whatsoever to do with Viget's core business. Some of them are truly pointless and Viget classifies them into, 'Tools, Experiments and Stunts.'

Viget CEO Brian williams lays out the ground rules for pointless projects in five succinct 'points'. He says:[93]

1. Anyone at Viget can spark an idea. That person then becomes the project champion.
2. The project champion 'pitches' the idea either at a Pointless Party (where interested folks come to discuss ideas and form

teams over pizza & beer) or just in the hallway. Pitching first means getting at least one other teammate involved (there are no solo Pointless Projects), then selling Andy and me (co-founders) on making it an 'official' Pointless Project.

3. Once official, the project has a slot on our weekly project schedule, just like any client. It also has deadlines.

4. Progress is shared at least weekly on our internal blog and during staff meetings.

5. Generally speaking, late nights are enjoyed by the team to hit deadlines. The projects are labours of love, and since client work (again, our point) takes precedence over Pointless Projects, we often have to find extra time to get them done.

So why do it? Pointless Corp gives all of Viget's talent opportunities to have fun together, be part of something cool and invest their ideas in Viget. This creates shared ideation and perhaps some intellectual capital too, which binds the group together. It also makes Viget an ideal platform or organization for some of the smartest talent to congregate.

Google, Pixar and Viget are great examples of big and small firms committed to creative freedom. But one company more than any other has been showing us the path for years.

CASE STUDY: 15 PER CENT TIME

3M began life as a failure. The Minnesota Mining and Manufacturing Company, as it was called at the time, was incorporated in 1902 by five founders looking to mine corundum, a key ingredient for sandpaper and grinding tools. But their first mine at Crystal Bay on the shores of Lake Superior was a major bust. Heavy in debt, the fledgling company tried several new ideas to survive. The second venture, a sandpaper mill, produced some of the poorest quality product in the market. It was years before 3M finally mastered the abrasive business and found steady customers in the booming automotive industry. The company had finally found a niche, yet it was only the beginning of a very successful journey. In the roaring 1920s, 3M took off on the back of a brand-new innovation—adhesive tapes. Dressed in Tartan packaging, 'Scotch' tape would set the benchmark for decades.

This was a company built on experimentation. One which recognized the dominant value of innovative products and new ideas. So in the late 1940s, as the dust of World War II had begun to settle, 3M's leaders were already thinking about how powerful a broad-based innovation culture could be in a new world thirsting for new products. In 1948, 3M introduced the '15% time' program. Every employee, not just the R&D folks, could use this time to develop ideas or even fancies which might help 3M one day. Sure, many 15% experiments failed, but others spectacularly did not.

In 1974, 3M chemical engineer Art Fry was looking to create a reusable bookmark for his church hymn book. Something that stuck securely yet did not leave a residue on the hymn book when removed. This was his 15% time challenge.[94]

Art had heard of a failed product that Dr Spencer Silver, a colleague of his at 3M, had developed in 1968. Called acrylate copolymer microspheres, this pressure sensitive adhesive was so weak it was thought to have no practical use. But importantly, it left no residue. Art got his hands on some of it, and with it, the first post-it note was born.

Even if not part of a formal policy like at 3M or Google, the best talent appreciates the time and space to work on their creative ideas. When an organization respects this need and allows for it, it communicates a deep intellectual trust to its talent. It says, 'We know and respect that you are more than just your job description.' Coupled with the learning motive described later, this is as powerful a retention magnet as any. It serves us well to remember that the most talented employees don't turn up just for a salary or to fulfil a routine need. They turn up bright-eyed because they have an idea in play.

2. ENTERPRISE AGILITY

In the previous chapter, we saw how VUCA circumstances could put businesses under tremendous pressure. This demands a nimble organization where the majority of the talent isn't locked down in narrow silos and blinkered by constricting job descriptions.

The relatively static nature of job specifications and job descriptions makes them a legacy of the so-called scientific management thinking from the first half of the 20th century. Built from time and motion studies in factory environments, detailed job specs don't translate well for knowledge work. For one, they reflect competence as was, not as could be. Two, as most are written by hiring managers when a role is first created, they suffer from heuristic and cognitive bias, that is, hiring managers often write them as a reflection of their own qualifications and experiences. As a hiring tool, this makes them even less useful and might even make them a hindrance to innovative approaches or thinking.

Most importantly, as performance and compensation are often tied to role expectations with annual review cycles, the use of static job descriptions severely limits the skill and role agility needed in dynamic markets.

Every body of work does have a few non-negotiables, both on the technical (what) and professional (how) side. We are clearly in an age when collaboration trumps structure. Overly detailed job descriptions can deepen functional isolation and limit the overall impact of perfectly good talent with strong transferable skills. Our goal instead should be to orient our talent system to value-creating outcomes. In an era of high talent mobility, the shift to team capability and collaborative work structures present a more practical way forward.

SQUARE WHEELS

At the start of my senior management programs, I sometimes show a picture to the audience's amusement (fig 10.2). After the chuckling has subsided, I remind them that a little restraint might be in order. After all, they might just be laughing at themselves!

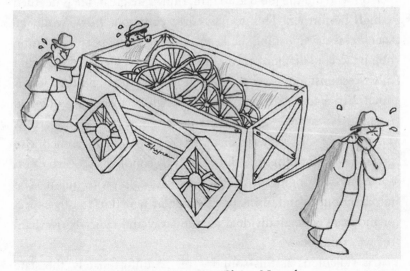

Illustration courtesy: Shyna Nagpal
Fig. 10.2: A Modern Organization: Hiring for Role

The situation in the picture is, sadly, quite common in the modern organization. Let's imagine for a moment that the two hard-working souls in the picture above represent a manager pulling the cart and a team member pushing it. From the sweat and exertion on their faces, both look to be trying very hard. Through heroic drudgery and doggedness, I would wager that the two probably get the cart to its destination in the end. And burn themselves out in the bargain.

Sounds familiar, doesn't it? Here's why it happens so often:

This cart was probably designed well before the two in the picture knew they would be pulling or pushing it. So when the gentleman at the back of the cart was selected, he was hired purely for his ability to push. That is his job description as well as the hiring profile for the job. This is a fairly common 'skills-based' selection scenario.

Once hired and trained, as long as he pushes harder than the person who did the job before him, things are great. He is deemed a high performer. This too is fairly common. Now while he spends his days pushing, he keeps looking at the person in front, hoping to land that job one day. Pulling involves less drudgery and more responsibility. You get to pick the direction and the view is much better too. As time passes, the high performing gentleman pushing the cart does get promoted. He is now pulling the cart. As a manager of sorts now, his first job is to hire and train someone to push the cart for him. And thus, the cycle continues for each of us. Far from questioning the status quo, we begin protecting it. The job descriptions and hiring profiles at play here don't really expect or motivate either individual to step away and radically overhaul the way things work.

As ridiculous as this sounds, this is, unfortunately, the state of affairs in a vast majority of businesses today, where success demands heroic effort, against the odds, rather than working with favourable odds. We can see symptoms all around us—in outdated supervision mindsets, farcical performance management discussions, meaningless ratings, restrictive and linear career paths, or a hundred other defunct practices which masquerade in the name of people management.

Equally, we all bear the consequences too, be it in historically low levels of employee engagement and loyalty, or in the historically high levels of work stress, uncertainty, burnout or depression.

THE COURAGE TO STEP AWAY

In the example of the two individuals I described above, I can't fault either of them. Human beings naturally resist change. We are prone to overstressing our belief in past competence and every new hire inherits a library of performance descriptors and standard operating procedures on day one.

Further, it is difficult to challenge the status quo and because we seldom step out of our role, many of us never spot that the answer to our problem may sit in the cart itself—the round tyres. All capability innovation comes from stepping away from the existing way of work and looking for faster, smarter and cheaper ways of generating better outcomes.

3. SHARED SUCCESS

The twin goals of greater autonomy and empowerment within a talent system also changes the meaning of management. The modern manager's reason for being has gone from a 'supervisor of task and outcomes' to an 'enabler of collective success'. To make this shift, he or she must give up the judge's robes for the coach's uniform. If employees don't succeed, managers are clearly on the line too.

A long-term mentor of mine and a world-leading applied behavioural science practitioner, Sushma Sharma, feels the only way managers can do this is by going from 'employee evaluation' to 'employee valuation'. Even Aubrey Daniels, the person behind the original performance management movement, was quite critical of how ratings and evaluation had hijacked the process in general. In his 2009 book *Oops: 13 Management Practices that Waste Time and Money*, Daniels called out the performance appraisal as the third (of thirteen) management practices that don't work. He said, 'No activity in corporate life is more universally despised by both managers and employees than performance appraisal.' According to Daniels, 'Several studies show that 80% of employees think they perform in the top 20% of the employed population. This means that at least 60% of employees, at any given time, are unhappy about the performance rating. So why do we put ourselves through it? Is it some sadistic ritual?'[95]

Yet, it took organizations well past 2011 to finally muster up enough courage to pull the plug on annual reviews and performance ratings. Consulting firms Deloitte, Accenture and Cap Gemini, along with software major Microsoft, were a few of the first in the Fortune 1000 to give up ratings, a move which caused quite a stir at the time. Since then, hundreds have followed suit, replacing the stressful annual performance cycle with feedback systems which are more immediate or near term, informal and objective. A 2014 CEB survey[96] found that across the Fortune 1000, 12 per cent of companies had ditched annual reviews. That number in 2012 was a bare 4 per cent. In 2015, the organization which pioneered so many people-practices in use today—General Electric—also killed their annual review system.

REAL TIME AND TECHNOLOGY ENABLED

Many big companies are using this transition away from annual review and rating cycles as a great opportunity to equip their managers with technology-enabled coaching platforms. These mobile app-based systems are way ahead of the old-fashioned, on-line performance management systems in common use so far, the main advantage being that they are built for in-the-moment and short-cycle performance coaching and feedback. No more waiting for months. Quick informal feedback sessions could be monthly, quarterly or scheduled on demand.

At GE, the system runs via a mobile app called PD@GE. Employees agree 'priorities' with their managers, who schedule 'touch-points'. Employees can request feedback from a host of people, including their managers, at any time, using a feature called 'insights'. The app can help capture discussion notes, pictures, recordings and is a real-time tool to help both employees and managers focus on real-time performance improvement. This is a huge step from the judgemental rating culture which drove GE for years.[97]

MANAGEMENT: FOR THE PEOPLE

It is easy to mistake the actions against ratings and top-down performance management as a recent phenomenon. While the deep discontent against ratings and appraisals in specific has existed for decades, what has made the simmering cauldron boil over is a much broader rejection of carrot-and-stick management culture as a whole. What worked in the factory now no longer works in the limitless multiverse of knowledge work.

As much as we try to brand the traditional performance appraisal a two-way dialogue, we cannot run away from the fact that at its core, the conversation is often one-way, top-down. And the best talent clearly wants more than a one-way viewpoint. For talent with in-demand skills, managers today must realize 'who is appraising whom'. With other job offers readily available, many employees enter a performance dialogue privately, considering if their current manager is worth another year of their career. In the future, if we want the performance feedback dialogue to survive, and perhaps even thrive, then the emphasis must be on honesty and true egalitarianism. In practice, this means managers only gain the right to give feedback when they first genuinely seek the same on their own performance as leaders. Not just through 360-degree reviews, but also through authentic conversations, asking, 'How am I performing as your manager?' and 'How can I help you succeed?' Only then can the conversation shift to, 'How you can improve' and 'This is what you should focus on'.

4. STRATEGIC FLEXIBILITY: INTEGRATING DYNAMIC CAPABILITY

Every Dynamic Capability Manager must design and publish a collaboration framework and operating footprint within a distributed team. Doing so helps resolve the inherent tension between individual needs (flexibility mobility or work-life outcomes) and organizational needs (co-located work, innovation or problem-solving). The primary driver of this decision is the specific talent recipe of a business, that is, the mix of internal, external and network capability employed.

This mix drives the specific architecture of locations, remote work and productivity tools which may be needed to meet both customer and shareholder needs. An organization may choose to locate some segments of its strategic talent in just two or three locations, for example, product teams at R&D laboratories or strategic sales teams in the same cities as the clients they manage.

At the same time, the same organization can be much more flexible with functional innovators, who serve a wide spectrum of internal customers and monitor external service delivery as well. For freelance or agency capabilities, greater flexibility raises the quality and quantity of talent we can access. The diagram in fig. 10.3 exemplifies how a management team can use design thinking to work through dynamic capability architecture.

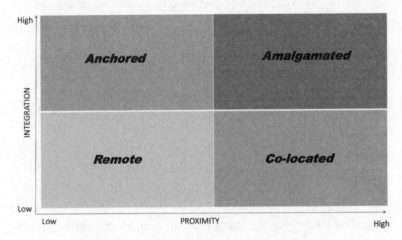

Fig. 10.3: Dynamic Capability Architecture

By plotting all sources of capability on this map, we can generate a view of how the flexibility of association and location currently works within the business. One example is in fig. 10.4.

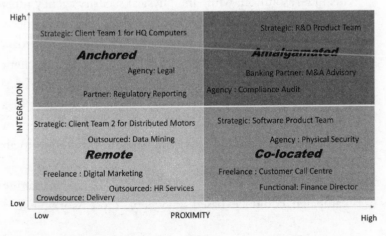

Fig. 10.4: Flexibility of Association and Location

As fig. 10.4 shows us:

1. *Internal Capabilities*
   ◆ While the R&D team must be co-located out of the central laboratories, other strategic talent, like the one designing software products, could have its members based out of any of the company's offices, keeping in mind network access, and code and data security.
   ◆ On the client side, the Client Team 1 may need to be based in the same city as the Client's HQ, for easy access to decision-makers, even if their employers don't have an office there. In contrast, Client Team 2, supporting a motor company with ten plants across the country, could be based anywhere and travel as needed.
   ◆ The finance function, in this case, must necessarily operate out of the same office as the P&L owner they support.

2. *External Capabilities*
   ◆ The legal firm this company uses should ideally be based in the jurisdiction used by the company for contracts and dispute resolution, while the physical security agency must be present in locations where the company has offices, factories and other physical assets. In contrast, the data security agency could be based anywhere. Lastly, a client may even expect external or agency talent to be based out of their offices when conducting a compliance check of a forensic audit. This prevents the unnecessary movement of files, records, electronic data and similar information to an offsite location.
   ◆ While freelance talent working on a digital marketing campaign could be based anywhere, those working in a

24-hour customer care centre, may need to turn up at an outsourced facility.

- If this firm needs delivery services for customers across the country, it could crowdsource individually-priced micro-jobs to individuals or delivery companies via an online workflow management application.

3. *Network Capabilities*

- An investment banking partner advising on a particularly tricky M&A deal could be co-located for a few months in the same city as the CEO or CFO.
- And outsourcing partners, involved in mining and scrubbing data or providing payroll and benefits services, could be located anywhere.

Rather than through policy and past practice, the distributed capability map allows you to look at flexibility in a nuanced yet common sense way. A Future-Ready Organization must embrace strategic flexibility and a fluid capability model, defined by its ability to move work across the ten pillars of dynamic capability.

In conclusion, accounting for the explosion of both talent and job mobility, we must aim to master the diversity of capability options that are now available. Our products are made from components which come from different parts of the world. Our services too can be delivered from anywhere today. It serves us well to imagine the future business unit as a connected ecosphere, and not just as roles on an organization chart.

11

BUILDING THE FUTURE-READY ORGANIZATION
Dynamic Capability Strategy

Strategy in its simplest form is nothing but the art of choice.
—*Gyan Nagpal*

THE DYNAMIC CAPABILITY TOOLKIT

Building and managing for the future requires a significant shift in culture away from industrial-era and scarcity-centric thinking. This is what the Chief Capability Strategist must achieve and, in doing so, carry the senior-most decision-makers in the organization along. A mentor of mine once told me that *organizations rise and fall on the strength of fifty people*. These fifty include the culture-shapers, the most visible role models and those who set the behavioural norms within an organization. Although many of them will occupy executive positions, it is important to note that not all need to be senior. It isn't uncommon to find well-networked middle managers with strong social capital in this group of fifty.

These culture-shapers understand and support the shift towards dynamic capability thinking and management. Rarely can a Chief Capability Strategist unwind decades of dogma, process or hierarchy without a powerful chorus for support.

Once acceptance and aspiration for Dynamic Capability Management exist, it becomes important to consciously map our current talent recipe today and then consciously orient future capability choices in the right direction. This is the Dynamic Capability Strategy.

STRATEGY IN ITS SIMPLEST FORM

Strategy in its simplest form is nothing but the art of choice. We all have access to limited resources—money, time, skills, and so on, yet we have unlimited ways to deploy them. Choosing the best application of our resources or energy must be the specific goal of our strategic ambitions.

This approach ensures a couple of outcomes. It reminds us of the inherent risks of making our strategy too complex. People may not understand what we are trying to achieve, may miss the wood for the trees, or underestimate execution dependencies as we implement. Keeping strategy simple and focused on a few critical outcomes helps us drive understanding, execution and hence success. The other advantage of framing strategic dialogue as the art of choice ensures that we achieve essential symmetry between our reality and imagination, protecting us from strategic overreach or even worse, an almost immoral lack of ambition.

In this chapter, we profile the four steps to build a future-ready talent system for a business. And no matter what we look like today, or how tactical our current capability agendas may be, by crossing these four thresholds in the right sequence, we can significantly transform how we access and utilize talent in the future. Let's go through each step in the correct sequence of deployment.

1. DISCOVER YOUR CURRENT TALENT RECIPE

Before taking the first step forward on any journey, it is important to know where exactly we are starting this journey from—what researchers call a 'baseline'. In this case, creating a baseline involves discovering your existing mix of capability across all nine pillars. As we saw in chapter 3, every organization today *already* uses dynamic capability in some shape or form. Industry level shifts and competitive pressures over the last thirty years have resulted in the virtual ubiquity of agencies, functional teams, outsourcing vendors, strategic partnerships, acquisitions and other similar capability choices. Without establishing a baseline today, it is improbable we can imagine what we may look like tomorrow.

When I present my research to executive teams and supervisory boards across the world, most CEOs are shocked and sometimes even mildly angry at themselves for not knowing what their current capability system looks like. Many have never even thought in this way, which is ironic because capability costs of all types dominate the expense side of the P&L statements they probably know by heart. This leads me to one of the most powerful outcomes of starting by discovering your current talent recipe—it provides nine firm and finite indices to calculate the demonstrable P&L impact of your future capability choices over the long term.

While our primary goals remain the enhancement of the organization's access to new types of skills and the evolution of our capability agendas for an age of digital business, we hope to do so in a manner which also makes the organization nimble, flexible and cost effective. On this last point, the effective implementation of dynamic capability strategy can save the company millions, by eliminating waste, and also add millions to income, through new sources of revenue. Demonstrating this impact is only possible once a firm baseline is established.

The process involved in researching and publishing your current talent recipe normally takes a couple of weeks of focused effort and requires a degree of collaboration and systems thinking. I would recommend you look at it as a seven-stage process:

1. Introduce the executive team to the Dynamic Capability Framework and interpret the principles and application within your industry (fig. 11.1).

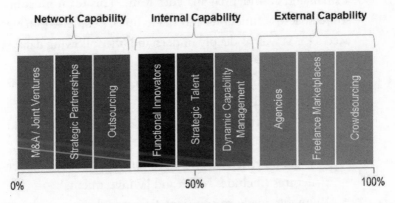

Fig. 11.1: Dynamic Capability Framework

It is important they see this as a shared exercise in building the organization for the long term. When I facilitate such sessions, I try and keep their focus on possibilities, rather than on constraints, costs and other similar challenges. It also helps to align the group to the specific industry forces which threaten disruption or drive the need for new skills and capabilities.

Our goal at this stage is to convert the executive team into supportive sponsors and at the same time, help manage any residual anxiety around introducing a new process. This anxiety is natural and normal. It stems from the risks of deep disclosure and perhaps from a fear of losing control over precious resources.

This is another reason why I always insist that only the CEO can play the role of the Chief Capability Strategist. It is the CEOs job, in this case, to ensure that the process of analyzing the organization's current capability architecture never descends into a witch-hunt for underutilized headcount or an inquisition into past capability choices. It must always be a discreet, strategic, collaborative and a 'feed-forward' exercise.

2. Once this is done, the next stage requires the assembly of a small and confidential analytics team. This team must be sourced across functions and made up of people who have access to, as well as deeply understand, the following data:
    * Current full-time employment numbers and costs
    * Current contract labour and part-time employment numbers and costs
    * Vendors profiles, contracts, service level agreements and costs
    * Key (strategic) relationships, subsidiaries and other structures (includes M&A and JV investments)
    * Payments made to transient talent, including agencies, consultants and project resources
    * Licence and deployment costs for new productivity enhancements, including software
    * Investments made in smart technology

I recommend this team have between four and seven senior members drawn from functions such as HR, finance, procurement, technology and business divisions, and it is important that the team be empowered and equipped with both time and access to ensure the projections they develop are as close to the truth as possible.

3. The first task this team must undertake is to map principal teams and roles within the organization to the nine pillars in the framework. This includes answering questions like— What does strategic talent mean within our business? Who are our value creators and our value retainers? What roles are purely supervisory or executive in nature? What types of vendor relationships or strategic partnerships form a part of the organization's distributed capability? How should we define the boundary between niche expertise (agency talent) and commoditized skills (marketplaces or crowdsourcing) within our external source pool?

4. At this stage, I recommend the analytics team validate their assumptions and present their internal hypotheses and definitions on each of the nine pillars to the executive team. This ensures all business leaders have a voice before the numbers are pulled from the financial system. Further, beyond just supporting the activity, all business and functional leaders might need to help the project team resolve more granular queries on cost or headcount allocations.

5. This brings us to the most critical stage of the whole process. The team must now begin the task of estimating both effort and cost across the organization's distributed talent landscape. At this stage, discretion and confidentiality are paramount and hence actions must be undertaken in a seamless deep-dive in the shortest possible time. Almost like an 'all-hands-on-deck' situation. I always recommend the team do both an aggregation of capability cost across all nine pillars of the Dynamic Capability Framework and, at the

same time, also estimate headcount numbers in each pillar. This will result in two distinct talent recipes—one by cost and the other by headcount. Both are powerful diagnostic insights for executive review. The illustration in fig. 11.2 is one such example which was compiled during the research phase of this book.

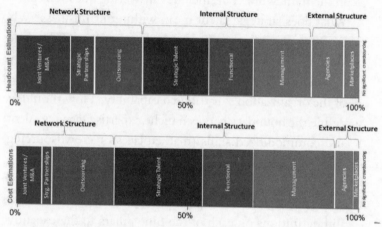

Fig. 11.2: Dynamic Capability Network: Cost and Headcount

In my experience, it is not uncommon to see employee costs and outsourcing costs dominate the hard expenditure view. Equally, the result may be skewed towards just a few pillars, with many pillars with negligible numbers or even none.

AVOID THE 'UNKNOWN' SHORTCUT

What must be avoided is the tendency to park numbers in a new 'unknown' or 'non-strategic talent' column. During one of our research conclaves, a large consumer goods company tried to do exactly this, placing 32 per cent of their overall talent in an unknown bucket. They defined these roles as 'execution' roles and hence not truly strategic to the business.

This is a dangerous temptation as it could wrongly signify a lower (or even lack of) importance for this resource. The goal at this stage of research is to first find the current capability equilibrium of the organization. We aren't necessarily looking for restructure targets or cost-saving opportunities. Hence, we must avoid hijacking leadership attention away from our primary goal. As if to prove this point, even at our research conclave, it was this unwanted fourth pillar within the internal structure which ended up dominating the debate.

I strongly suggest the research team make an informed assumption of where these hard-to-define roles must sit within the three internal capability pillars and record these assumptions in an annexure of sorts, for further scrutiny if required.

6. It is also important to know when to stop analyzing. I recommend a minimum data threshold of 85 per cent. In other words, our goal should be to capture at least 85 per cent of headcount and spend within a single capability bucket, if not more. I have found that often the task of uncovering the last 15 per cent can take as much time as the first 85 per cent and hence may not be worth the extra time. The impact of this final 15 per cent may not materially skew the overall capability ratios at all.

DEALING WITH HIDDEN HEADCOUNT

Often, a cost-based exercise such as this uncovers a few hidden headcount in the form of interns, contractors and other off-the-employment-ledger talent. This number should usually be quite small and can be clubbed with other contingent roles in the freelancer bucket. If the number is quite large, this may indicate large-scale employment abuse or some other fraud.

The research team must now present their findings, along with the assumptions made, to the executive committee for their comments and final approval. Finally, I recommend the research team also conduct a post-mortem review of sorts and record how they went about their task. This guidance document can prove critical to the next team which attempts this activity, twelve or twenty-four months hence.

2. DIAGNOSE TALENT RISK AND OPPORTUNITIES

The second step to achieve a Future-Ready Organization powered by dynamic capability is to build an outside-in perspective on capability itself; in specific, how the overall marketplace for capability is evolving. Taking an outside-in approach forces us to appreciate how business and society are evolving and how this evolution affects our future talent choices. This also hedges against the common mistake of building strategy which is too inward-looking or focused on just our current challenges. Insular (inside-out) approaches often result in a change-resistant organization which grows in its own image or reflection.

TALENT SYSTEM DIAGNOSIS

There are literally hundreds of shifts in motion within any local talent system, at any given point in time. Some are transitory and are driven by short-term swings, like economic booms or recessions. Other are more permanent and mirror a systemic shift, like steep changes in technology or evolving work preferences.

Like in any good and sound exercise, it is important to first get a broad spectrum of relevant perspectives on the table. Over the two years it took to research and write this book, my team and

I facilitated twenty-three focus groups to gather our metadata on capability trends. These focus groups were made up of a diverse spectrum of business and HR leaders across Asia, Africa and Europe. I would try and run them on the back of every executive workshop I conducted, and they all followed exactly the same template:

1. We started by asking each group of well-heeled business leaders to list and analyze the big capability shifts they were witnessing within their geography or industry. The answers that came back invariably ranged from the seismic (AI and robotics disrupting jobs) to the tactical (maternity leave legislation or monetization of employee benefits).
2. Once a core list of around twenty key trends had been established in each location, we asked the leaders to rate each trend on two core dimensions:
   a. The *difficulty* a specific trend posed to their business.
   b. The *degree of control* they perceived their organization had in responding to a trend.

You will recognize the two variables of difficulty and control from the VUCA framework we discussed in chapter 8. We used them deliberately to analyze the kinds of responses possible on each talent risk. Many of my personal learnings from this talent trend mapping exercise ended up in forming the twelve strategic responses to VUCA we reviewed earlier.

Coming back to trends, the plot in fig. 11.3 represents the final distillate from the metadata we received across all twenty-three focus groups. Representing them on the axis of relative difficulty and relative control helps add some executive flavour to each capability shift within a business circumstance.

Fig. 11.3: Talent Risk Metadata from Focus Groups

As you can see from fig. 11.3, the interplay of difficulty and control results in two broad types of capability shifts. Non-structural shifts are easier to work with and resolve. Being lower in difficulty and higher in control, these can be dealt with within the existing framework of practices an organization uses to manage capability. Hence, we can respond by changes in policies or by investing in making our talent processes or programmes more mature.

Structural shifts (relatively high difficulty and lower control) denote fundamental changes to a talent system. They represent changing philosophies in how we recognize, unlock and deploy capability within organizations. In these cases, our existing policy frameworks may prove inadequate in resolving these changes. What is needed instead is a more systemic response.

WHAT IS RISK?

It would be fallacious to label each of the shifts on Fig. 11.3 as a talent risk. Each one, indeed, could be interpreted as an opportunity as much as a risk to our current capability strategy. Identifying a shift as a risk is as much a function of context as it is of operating choices made in the past. For instance, if a capability shift aligns well with our overall business strategy or if it gives us an advantage over other competitors in our industry, then this is much more of an opportunity than a risk to our business. On the other hand, if a trend fundamentally challenges our existing business model, or if our culture is resistant to change, then this poses a significant risk to our success. And perhaps even our survival.

It is entirely possible that two competitors in the same industry may perceive the same shift differently. Here are three examples:

♦ The rise in the gig economy is as much an opportunity for Uber as it is a risk for the local taxi company looking for drivers on fixed shifts.

♦ A healthcare or pharma company may see societal ageing as an opportunity, whereas for a lifestyle brand geared to the young, this may be a significant risk.

♦ Trends showing an increase in workplace flexibility and virtual working may be seen as a huge risk for a commercial real estate company, yet may be seen as a significant opportunity by a company which currently leases a lot of expensive office space.

Hence, opportunities and risk are both contextual. In either case, it is important that business executives are aware of how the overall ecosystem of capability surrounding their business is changing, and more important, how this change impacts their current set of talent choices.

Once we have mapped the shifts as we see them, we can identify those which pose the most significant risks to our business. In most cases, these risks are localized and domestic in nature. To help explain the localized nature of risk, here are four geographical risk maps which emerged from our focus groups with business executives (figs. 11.4, 11.5, 11.6 and 11.7):

Fig. 11.4: Talent Risks: India

Fig. 11.5: Talent Risks: UK

Talent Risks: Southern Africa

High

Degree of control

New age E.V.P.s

Non structural

Academic quality
Grad quality / faculty

Re-education/ skills

Flexi-work

Digital economy

Skill Shortages
Financial services / engineering / technology

Healthcare cost

Localization
v/s expatriation

Value based reward

Formative education quality
Teach/St Ratios / pass rate

Structural

Micro entrepreneurship

Political stability

Retention

Technological access

Low

Low — Degree of difficulty — High

Fig. 11.6: Talent Risks: Southern Africa

Talent Risks: UAE & GCC

High

Degree of control

Non structural

Reputation
Of company / country
for international talent

Economic climate

Education/ skills

Localization
Emiratization /Saudization
/Qatar/Oman

Regulation
Saudi - Taxes / Visas

Gender
Participation

Cyber security

Oil reserves
petrochemicals / proven
/ environmental impact /
regulations

Structural

Ageing

Low

Low — Degree of difficulty — High

Fig. 11.7: Talent Risks: UAE & GCC

Each risk map was the result of many local leaders debating and agreeing capability trends which threatened business success at a local level. These were nuanced conversations and, as you can see, even when the same risk was highlighted across several markets— like skills shortages—the underlying reason was different. In Britain, executives in our focus group worried about a shortage of local talent opting for careers in science, technology, engineering and maths (STEM), while in Africa, the conversation highlighted the debilitating shortages of local talent with the right skills being felt by the banking, manufacturing, telecom and IT industries. In India, the focus was on the poor quality of academics in higher education and the poor skill levels within professionals, managers, executives and technicians (PMET) across several industry segments.

BUILD YOUR TALENT RISK MAP

The evidence collected highlights the need for all business leaders to be acutely aware of the major talent risks surrounding their business. This should be one of the inputs into future capability strategy. To help you build a customized view for your organization, I have enclosed a blank chart in fig 11.8. As you fill this up, think about how your industry is changing and how customer expectations from your business are evolving. The meta-trends map (fig. 11.3) and country risk maps (figs. 11.4 to 11.7) are a good starting point, but you could choose to go far beyond this list and much deeper, based on your specific location or business model. The goal should be to interpret changes to our talent recipe being driven by corresponding changes in customer needs, technology or competition. Also, think about skill issues facing your industry as a whole. Is it harder to find and keep some types of talent?

If your readiness on a key trend is weak, this could be a risk for you. Involve others in the dialogue to get different and multifaceted opinions on the table.

Once you have identified between seven and twelve risks, consider where you stand on both the x and y-axis of this chart. What is the degree of difficulty your organization faces on each talent risk? How much control do you have, as you respond to this risk? Use this collective perspective to create your own talent risk map in fig. 11.8.

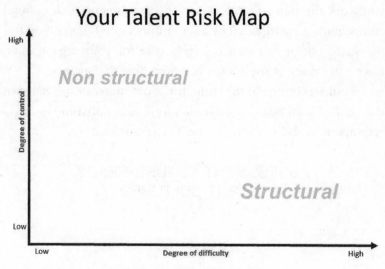

Fig. 11.8: Your Own Talent Risk Map: Blank

3. DIAGNOSE YOUR CULTURE

The third step (and final diagnosis viewpoint) focuses on your organization's future readiness. As we have seen in previous chapters, almost everyone already uses distributed capability sources in some shape or form. However, we do so in a disconnected and tactical manner. What this means, in consequence, is that while some parts of our business or our culture are already starting to change and mature, other parts may still lag. This is why a cultural diagnosis can prove handy. Before investing a single dollar in dynamic capability strategies, it is important that we identify both the headwinds and tailwinds which exist within our existing belief system.

There are ten cultural competencies which correlate strongly with the adoption and eventual success of a distributed capability ecosystem. The following simple diagnostic assessment helps you work through all ten areas. In this assessment, each cultural competence is exemplified by a set of direct questions. If you feel the statement or question is largely true for your organization, place a tick mark in the answer box preceding the question.

I would recommend the entire list of questions are answered in one go. If you know the organization well, your initial and intuitive response is probably the right one. Let's get started.

ASSESSMENT: FUTURE-READY TALENT CULTURES

1. *Culture of Sharing*

☐ In our organization, we enjoy working on cross-functional projects.

☐ The sharing of headcount and resources across business lines is encouraged.

☐ We have a mature internal mobility policy.

☐ Career mobility between business divisions (revenue) and support functions (HR, finance, marketing, etc.) is encouraged.

☐ The atmosphere across different lines of business is collaborative.

☐ We follow an open and transparent approach when solving problems.

2. *Culture of Ideation and Innovation*

☐ In our organization, we often experiment with new ideas.

☐ When trying new things, we have a high tolerance for failure.

☐ Our innovation agenda is driven by the voice of the customer.

☐ Our approach to experimentation is quick and iterative.

☐ Our project management methodology is AGILE.

3. *Culture of Analytics*

☐ Our senior leaders are data savvy.

☐ Our data quality is generally clean, accurate and reliable.

☐ We have access to industry-leading capabilities in data modelling.

☐ Our managers are skilled at working with dashboards and scorecards.

☐ Our decisions are driven by real-time analytics.

4. *Outside-in Thinking*

☐ We are the thought leaders in our industry.

☐ We actively study industry trends and developments.

☐ We buy new intellectual property to supplement internal product development.

☐ Our digital security systems are best in class.

☐ Our data protection protocols are best in class.

5. *Automation*

☐ In our industry, we are an early adopter of automation.
☐ We have an Artificial Intelligence adoption plan.
☐ Our automation efforts are led cross-functionally (not just by the IT department).

6. *Partnership Culture*

☐ We have more than one strategic partnership driving customer value.
☐ We see organizations supplying us services as partners (as opposed to vendors).
☐ We have a history of successful joint ventures.
☐ Our partners give us frequent feedback on how we are supporting their success.
☐ Our evaluation systems for existing partners are robust.

7. *Expertise Development*

☐ Our investments in building in-house capability are best in the industry.
☐ We have a rich group of external experts we can rely on for support.

8. *Management Culture*

☐ Our management incentives are primarily based on organizational performance (as opposed to individual performance).
☐ Our managers receive regular and confidential feedback from peers.

☐ Our managers receive regular and confidential feedback from external stakeholders (customers, suppliers, partners).

☐ Our managers receive regular and confidential feedback from their team.

☐ We have consistent project management and project reporting standards.

☐ Our managers are trained in project management and reporting.

☐ Our managers have expertise in finding and managing distributed capability.

9. *Architecture*

☐ Our organization structure is fluid and responsive to market changes.

☐ We actively promote a mix of top-down, peer-to-peer and bottom-up accountability.

10. *Talent Culture*

☐ We track employee engagement and satisfaction at work (monthly or quarterly).

☐ We have a culture of continuous and shared learning.

☐ We map and stay connected with our alumni.

☐ We encourage flexi-work and flexible career structures.

☐ Our employees can customize the benefits available to them.

☐ We have strong policies and programmes to support career mobility and growth.

Once you complete all forty-six questions, what you should have in front of you is a checklist of your organization's strengths.

Every check-mark represents an area where you are (or tending towards being) future-ready.

Now examine the questions you left blank. They represent the areas which may hold you back from building a vibrant, dynamic capability culture. If we go back to my earlier definition of strategy as nothing more than 'the art of choice', then this assessment is a powerful tool in helping you prioritize and choose the investments which move you forward.

The right way to deploy this tool is to use it as a framework for executive debate and alignment. Get all your senior leaders to take this assessment. Analyze their check-marks, present it back to them and facilitate a dialogue to validate if the averages truly represent organizational reality.

I often analyze the data that emerges from such an executive pool for possible pockets of unity or divergence in thinking. For example, do senior executives in corporate headquarters see the organization in the same way as those in local business units or factories? Equally, do revenue earning divisions concur with support functions? Do all locations report a similar distributed talent culture? Or will some need significantly more investments in remodelling than others?

This insight can be a powerful ally in anchoring a meaningful strategy debate, as well as ensuring we aren't wasting precious resources—time and money—on the wrong agendas or locations. Smart strategy must guide scarce resources to the parts of the business that need them most.

CULTURE BALANCE SHEETS

Examining your culture is an important step in dynamic capability strategy, mainly because executives rarely get an opportunity to step away and look at the square wheels within their own culture.

Many see themselves, rightfully, as protectors and evangelists of the company's current culture. Very few recognize an organization's culture for what it truly is—a double-edged sword.

In linear times, an organization's culture is its greatest asset. However, in exponential and disruptive times, some parts of that same culture can become large liabilities, creating persistent resistance to pressing change and renewal.

Hence, disruptive times demand that the executive radar be well-tuned to practices within our culture which no longer work. Some parts of culture will remain an asset and must be fiercely protected. Others may have turned into toxic liabilities which threaten our very existence.

Tools such as this assessment help you identify what needs to be changed. The boxes ticked, versus those left blank, are effectively a 'balance sheet' of your culture system.

4. BUILD A 2025 HYPOTHESIS

With diagnosis done, it is now time to turn an eye to the future. And visualize what an organization could look like in the future if it embraced a dynamic and flexible capability system.

We have already seen in chapter 3 that this is not an option anymore. It is necessary. Even if we don't choose to change, industry level shifts, changing consumer preferences, new digital capabilities and most important of them all, disruptive competitors who look radically different to us will force this change upon us.

The ultimate goal of our talent strategy is to arrive at the ideal talent recipe for our business over the next strategy cycle—a capability sweet-spot, which maximizes flexibility and access to skill, while simultaneously minimizing waste and cost.

WHAT IS YOUR IDEAL TALENT RECIPE?

This sounds like a simple enough question for executives with intimate knowledge of the business. However, in my experience, the first time you try and answer it can prove challenging. The challenge isn't intellectual but emotional. Arriving at a common answer to this question can also be a deeply cathartic process because of three specific mental barriers that this process dismantles:

Firstly, it forces all executives to collectively buy into one big picture. Remember, we cannot answer this question unless we are willing to see the organization as a composite whole, as opposed to seeing it as a network of functional silos. This approach automatically prioritizes strategy over expertise and the needs of the customer over the structural needs of a hierarchy. We can organize and execute knowledge work in so many new ways today, be it by project teams, partnerships, shared services or automation. Equally, we can access expertise in whole new ways too, without owning or employing it full-time.

Another reason is that it forces executives to share rather than hoard resources. This isn't their fault entirely, especially if they have grown roots in cultures which reward individual performance with career success. Such leaders tend to place self-interest over the needs of the group, a situation which directly results in the power-centres and fiefdoms which traditional organization structures encourage.

Lastly, working together on building a future talent recipe for the business forces leaders to think creatively. When I am facilitating dynamic capability design labs, I split the executive group into cross-functional groups and assign them the same task—'Design a competitor for your business—the most ruthless and efficient competitor you can imagine, unencumbered by history and other constraints.' As they go about doing this, I also remind them that,

'For the next hour or so, forget you work in the company you do, but bring everything you know about the industry and customer to the table.'

Most presentations which follow are both radical and creative. The fictional designs are often more cost-effective and quite different from the organization that employs the group.

I often close with an invitation. 'If this is what we could potentially look like today, what should we look like in five years?'

NOTES

1. Brad Stone, Steve Jobs, 'The Return, 1997–2011', *Bloomberg Businessweek*, 7 October 2011,
   http://www.bloomberg.com/bw/magazine/the-return-19972011-10062011.html#p2.
2. Benj Edwards, 'The iPod: How Apple's Legendary Portable Music Player Came to Be', *Macworld*, 23 October 2011,
   http://www.macworld.com/article/1163181/ipods/the-birth-of-the-ipod.html.
   Also see, Sam Costello, 'This is the Number of iPods Sold All-Time', *Lifewire*, 13 October 2015, updated 7 May 2018,
   https://www.lifewire.com/number-of-ipods-sold-all-time-1999515.
3. Keza Macdonald, 'IGN Presents: The History of ATARI', 21 March 2014,
   http://www.ign.com/articles/2014/03/20/ign-presents-the-history-of-atari?page=2.
4. Tim Biggs, How Atari's Nolan Bushnell turned down Steve Jobs' offer of a third of Apple at $50,000, *The Sydney Morning Herald*, 24 March 2015,

https://www.smh.com.au/technology/how-ataris-nolan-bushnell-turned-down-steve-jobs-offer-of-a-third-of-apple-at-50000-20150324-1m62cm.html

5. Urvaksh Karkaria, 'Wozniak: "I begged HP to make the Apple I. Five times they turned me down" ', *Atlanta Business Chronicle*, 31 January 2013, http://www.bizjournals.com/atlanta/blog/atlantech/2013/01/wozi-begged-h-p-to-make-the-apple-1.html.

6. Josh Ong, 'Apple co-founder offered first computer design to HP 5 times', *Apple Insider*, 6 December 2010, http://appleinsider.com/articles/10/12/06/apple_co_founder_offered_first_computer_design_to_hp_5_times.

7. Steve Levy, *In the Plex: How Google Thinks, Works, and Shapes Our Lives* (New York: Simon and Schuster, 2011).

8. Peter F. Drucker, 'The New Society of Organizations', *Harvard Business Review*, September–October 1992, https://hbr.org/1992/09/the-new-society-of-organizations.

9. Jeff Loucks, James Macaulay, Andy Noronha, Michael Wade, *Digital Vortex: How Digital Disruption Is Redefining Industries* (Global Center for Digital Business Transformation, June 2015).

10. James Manyika, Gary Pinkus, Sree Ramaswamy, 'The Most Digital Companies Are Leaving All the Rest Behind', *Harvard Business Review*, 21 January 2016, https://hbr.org/2016/01/the-most-digital-companies-are-leaving-all-the-rest-behind.

11. Peter F. Drucker, 2008. *The Essential Drucker: The Best of Sixty Years of Peter Drucker's Essential Writings on Management* (New York: Collins Business Essentials, 2008).

12. Gyan Nagpal, *Talent Economics: The Fine Line between Winning and Losing the Global War for Talent* (London: Kogan Page, 2013).

13. 'Fit for the Future: Capitalising on Global Trends', *17th Annual CEO Survey*, PWC 2014, https://www.pwc.com/gx/en/ceo-survey/2014/assets/pwc-17th-annual-global-ceo-survey-jan-2014.pdf.

14. Lisa Beyer, 'The Rise and Fall of Employer-Sponsored Pension Plans', *Workforce*, 24 January 2012, http://www.workforce.com/2012/01/24/the-rise-and-fall-of-employer-sponsored-pension-plans/.

15. 'Private Pension Plan Bulletin Historical Tables and Graphs 1975–2016', Employee Benefits Security Administration, United States Department of Labor, December 2018, Version 1.0, https://www.dol.gov/sites/default/files/ebsa/researchers/statistics/retirement-bulletins/private-pension-plan-bulletin-historical-tables-and-graphs.pdf.

16. Michael Hammer, 'Reengineering Work: Don't Automate, Obliterate', *Harvard Business Review*, July–August 1990, https://hbr.org/1990/07/reengineering-work-dont-automate-obliterate.

17. Michael Hammer and James Champy, *Reengineering the Corporation: A Manifesto for Business Revolution* (New York: HarperBusiness, 1993).

18. Peter F. Drucker, 'The New Society of Organizations', *Harvard Business Review*, September–October 1992, https://hbr.org/1992/09/the-new-society-of-organizations.

19. Davan Maharaj, 'In the 1990s, Layoffs Become a Business Strategy', *The Seattle Times*, 13 December 1998, http://community.seattletimes.nwsource.com/archive/?date=19981213&slug=2788818.

20. Edmund L. Andrews, 'Job Cuts at AT&T Will Total 40,000, 13% of Its Staff', *The New York Times*, 3 January 1996, http://www.nytimes.com/1996/01/03/business/job-cuts-at-at-t-will-total-40000-13-of-its-staff.html.

21. Newsweek Staff, 'The Case Against Layoffs: They Often Backfire', *Newsweek*, 4 February 2010, https://www.newsweek.com/case-against-layoffs-they-often-backfire-75039.

22. 'State of the American Workplace, 2013,' Gallup Inc.,

http://www.gallup.com/file/services/176708/State_of_the_American_Workplace_.

23. 'Nearly One-Third of Employers Expect Workers to Job-Hop', *Career Builder*, 15 May 2015, http://www.careerbuilder.com/share/aboutus/pressreleasesdetail.aspx?sd=5%2F15%2F2014&id=pr824&ed=12%2F31%2 F2014.

24. Allison Schnidman et al., '2016 Global Talent Trends', LinkedIn, https://business.linkedin.com/content/dam/me/business/en-us/talent-solutions/resources/pdfs/2016-global-talent-trends-v4.pdf.

25. 'Declining Employee Loyalty: A Casualty of the New Workplace', *Knowledge@Wharton*, 9 May 2012, http://knowledge.wharton.upenn.edu/article/declining-employee-loyalty-a-casualty-of-the-new-workplace/.

26. 'Empowerment in a Disrupted World', *Mercer Global Talent Trends Study 2017*, Mercer Consulting, https://www.mercer.com/our-thinking/career/global-talent-hr-trends.html.

27. 'Rewriting the Rules for the Digital Age', *2017 Deloitte Global Human Capital Trends*, Deloitte University Press, https://www2.deloitte.com/content/dam/Deloitte/us/Documents/human-capital/hc-2017-global-human-capital-trends-us.pdf.

28. 'Visible Light and the Electromagnetic Spectrum', Source: Nasa https://www.nasa.gov/audience/forstudents/k-4/dictionary/Electromagnetic_Spectrum.html.

29. Julian Stodd, 'An Introduction to Scaffolded Social Learning', 30 October 2015, https://julianstodd.wordpress.com/2015/10/30/an-introduction-to-scaffolded-social-learning/.

30. Eleazar David Melendez, 'Financial Crisis Cost Tops $22 Trillion, GAO Says', *Huffpost*, 15 February 2013, https://www.huffingtonpost.com/2013/02/14/financial-crisis-cost-gao_n_2687553.html.

31. Paul Goydan and Henning Streubel, 'The Role of Support Functions in Upstream Value Creation', 20 November 2013,

https://www.bcg.com/publications/2013/energy-environment-role-support-functions-upstream-value-creation.aspx.

32. 'Holacracy and Self-Organization', *Zappos Insights*, https://www.zapposinsights.com/about/holacracy.

33. 'Morning Star's Success Story: No Bosses, No Titles, No Structural Hierarchy', *Corporate Rebels*, 14 November 2016, https://corporate-rebels.com/morning-star/.

34. Jim Highsmith, 'History: The Agile Manifesto', 2001, http://agilemanifesto.org/history.html.

35. Martin Fowler and Jim Highsmith, 'The Agile Manifesto', *Dr. Dobbs*, 1 August 2001, http://www.drdobbs.com/open-source/the-agile-manifesto/184414755.

36. 'Freelancing in America 2017', *Upwork*, https://www.upwork.com/i/freelancing-in-america/2017/.

37. 'How to Live the Freelance Life: Lessons From 1,000 Independents', Freelancers Union, 2014, https://fu-web-storage-prod.s3.amazonaws.com/content/filer_public/8f/d7/8fd7d4ce-f714-486e-b2d5-80e190b0ce70/fu_surveyinfographics_workandlife_v3.pdf.

38. 'Contingent Workforce: Size, Characteristics, Earnings, and Benefits', US Government Accountability Office, 20 April 2015, https://www.gao.gov/assets/670/669899.pdf.

39. James Manyika, Susan Lund, Jacques Bughin, Kelsey Robinson, Jan Mischke and Deepa Mahajan, 'Independent Work: Choice, Necessity and the Gig Economy', McKinsey Global Institute, October 2016, https://www.mckinsey.com/global-themes/employment-and-growth/independent-work-choice-necessity-and-the-gig-economy.

40. 'Empowerment in a Disrupted World', *Mercer Global Talent Trends Study 2017*, Mercer Consulting, https://www.mercer.com/our-thinking/career/global-talent-hr-trends.html.

41. 'Twenty Trends That Will Shape the Next Decade', Intuit 2020 Report, October 2010, http://http-download.intuit.com/http.intuit/CMO/intuit/futureofsmallbusiness/intuit_2020_report.pdf.

42. 'Why an Ex-Google Coder Earns Twice as Much Freelancing', Bloomberg, *Today*, 21 January 2016, https://www.todayonline.com/tech/why-ex-google-coder-earns-twice-much-freelancing.

43. Jack Neff, 'Tongal Is No. 10 on Ad Age's 2017', *AdAge India*, 2 January 2017, http://adage.com/article/special-report-agency-alist-2017/tongal-10-ad-age-s-2017-agency-a-list/307580/.

44. Tonyj, 'What is the ROI on Crowdsourcing with Topcoder?' 23 May 2016, https://www.topcoder.com/blog/what-is-the-roi-on-crowdsourcing-with-topcoder/.

45. 'Disability Inclusion', World Bank, updated 26 September 2018, http://www.worldbank.org/en/topic/disability.

46. 'Babysitter Survey', April 17, 2017, Care.com, https://www.care.com/press-release-carecom-releases-2017-babysitter-survey-results-p1186-q88331797.html.

47. Sandy Carter, Susanne Hupfer, 'Raising the Game: The IBM Business Tech Trends Study', IBM Center for Applied Insights, August 2014, https://www.google.com/url?sa=t&rct=j&q=&esrc=s&source=web&cd=3&cad=rja&uact=8&ved=2ahUKEwiKoMHOxp7hAhVJto8KHcqmAsIQFjACegQIAhAC&url=https%3A%2F%2Fwww.ibm.com%2Fdeveloperworks%2Fcommunity%2Ffiles%2Fbasic%2Fanonymous%2Fapi%2Flibrary%2F087482e3-c559-4919-9af1-61564eb247a3%2Fdocument%2Fb4720f97-63a1-46bb-904b-b8151c295925%2Fmedia&usg=AOvVaw3l-F7nrw2T0DmZgE-uPEhQ.

48. 'Wilshire 5000 Total Market Index', 31 March 2017,

https://wilshire.com/indexinfo/pdf/Wilshire%205000/
Wilshire%205000%20Fact%20Sheet.pdf.

49. 'Dealogic Data Shows 2015 M&A Volume Surpasses $5 Trillion'
CISION PR Newswire, 28 December 2015,
http://www.prnewswire.com/news-releases/dealogic-data-shows-
2015-ma-volume-surpasses-5-trillion-300197391.html.

50. 'Disney's Acquisition of Pixar', ICMR, IBS Center for
Management Research, 2006,
http://www.icmrindia.org/casestudies/catalogue/Business%20
strategy/BSTR203.htm.

51. Jay Walker, 'The Real Patent Crisis Is Stifling Innovation', Forbes,
18 June 2014,
https://www.forbes.com/sites/
danielfisher/2014/06/18/13633/#3bf65b8b6f1c.

52. Edward Jung, 'A Better Way from R to D', Project Syndicate, 27
April 2017,
https://www.project-syndicate.org/commentary/broken-
innovation-finance-system-by-edward-jung-2017-04.

53. Robert Weisman, 'Cost of Bringing Drug to Market Tops $2.5b,
Research Finds', The Boston Globe, 18 November 2014,
http://www.bostonglobe.com/business/2014/11/18/cost-bringing-
prescription-drug-market-tops-billion-tufts-research-center-
estimates/6mPph8maRxzcvftWjr7HUN/story.html.

54. Melissa Palmer, 'What Is a FlexPod?' NetApp, 19 May 2016,
https://blog.netapp.com/blogs/what-is-a-flexpod/.

55. Sandy Carter, Susanne Hupfer, 'Raising the Game: The IBM
Business Tech Trends Study', IBM Center for Applied Insights,
August 2014,
https://www.google.com/url?sa=t&rct=j&q=&esrc=s&source=
web&cd=3&cad=rja&uact=8&ved=2ahUKEwiKoMHOxp7hA
hVJto8KHcqmAsIQFjACegQIAhAC&url=https%3A%2F%2Fw
ww.ibm.com%2Fdeveloperworks%2Fcommunity%2Ffiles%2Fbasi
c%2Fanonymous%2Fapi%2Flibrary%2F087482e3-c559-4919-9af1-

61564eb247a3%2Fdocument%2Fb4720f97-63a1-46bb-904b-b8151c
295925%2Fmedia&usg=AOvVaw3l-F7nrw2T0DmZgE-uPEhQ.

56. C.K. Prahalad and Gary Hamel, 'The Core Competence of the
Corporation', *Harvard Business Review*, May–June 1990,
https://hbr.org/1990/05/the-core-competence-of-the-
corporation.

57. Charles Duhigg & Keith Bradsher, 'How US Lost Out on iPhone
Work', *The New York Times*, 21 January 2012,
https://www.nytimes.com/2012/01/22/business/apple-america-
and-a-squeezed-middle-class.html.

58. Jane Wakefield, 'Foxconn Replaces 60,000 Factory Workers with
Robots', BBC NEWS, 25 May 2016,
http://www.bbc.com/news/technology-36376966.

59. Phil Fersht, 'Indian IT to Shed Half a Million Jobs by 2021', *Factor
Daily*, 15 February 2017,
https://factordaily.com/indian-it-job-cuts-reskilling-automation/.

60. Daron Acemoglu, Pascual Restrepo, 'Robots and Jobs: Evidence
from US Labor Markets', 17 March 2017,
https://www.nber.org/papers/w23285.

61. Greg Ip, 'We Survived Spreadsheets, and We'll Survive AI', *The
Wall Street Journal*, 2 August 2017,
https://www.wsj.com/articles/wesurvived-spreadsheets-and-well-
survive-ai-1501688765.

62. ibid.

63. Alan Dawson, 'Roger Federer Said He Wouldn't Be as Successful
Without Rafa Nadal—Here's Why', *Business Insider*, 25 May 2018,
https://www.businessinsider.sg/roger-federer-wouldnt-be-as-
successful-without-rafa-nadal-2018-5/?r=US&IR=T.

64. Daron Acemoğlu and Pascual Restrepo, 'The Race Between
Machine and Man: Implications of Technology for Growth,
Factor Shares and Employment', *VOX CEPR Policy Portal*, 5 July
2016,
http://voxeu.org/article/job-race-machines-versus-humans.

65. Herbert Alexander Simon, *Models of Man: Social and Rational-Mathematical Essays on Rational Human Behaviour in a Social Setting* (New York: J. Wiley, 1957).

66. Herbert A. Simon, speaker, 'Designing Organizations for an Information-Rich World', https://digitalcollections.library.cmu.edu/awweb/awarchive?type=file&item=33748.

67. Jason Dana, 'The Utter Uselessness of Job Interviews', *The New York Times*, 8 April 2017, https://mobile.nytimes.com/2017/04/08/opinion/sunday/the-utter-uselessness-of-job-interviews.html?smid=tw-share&referer=https%3A%2F%2Ft.co%2FKLnbelPvWZ.

68. Tom Simonite, 'Robot Journalist Finds New Work on Wall Street', *MIT Technology Review*, 9 January 2015, https://www.technologyreview.com/s/533976/robot-journalist-finds-new-work-on-wall-street/.

69. Nisha Ramchandani, 'The Rise and Rise of Chatbots', *The Business Times*, 16 October 2017, http://www.businesstimes.com.sg/technology/the-rise-and-rise-of-chatbots.

70. A.G. Lafley, 'What Only the CEO Can Do', *The Harvard Business Review*, May 2009, https://hbr.org/2009/05/what-only-the-ceo-can-do.

71. Tim Harford, 'How Department Stores Changed the Way We Shop', *BBC NEWS*, 14 August 2017. https://www.bbc.com/news/business-40448607.

72. Peter F. Drucker, *Management: Tasks, Responsibilities, Practices* (New York: Harper & Row, 1974).

73. J.M. Juran and F.M. Gryna, *Juran's Quality Control Handbook*, (New York: McGraw-Hill, 1951).

74. Jim L. Smith, 'Management: The Lasting Legacy of the Modern Quality Giants', *Quality Magazine*, 6 October 2011,

http://www.qualitymag.com/articles/88493-management--the-lasting-legacy-of-the-modern-quality-giants.

75. 'Staying One Step Ahead at Pixar: An Interview with Ed Catmull', *McKinsey Quarterly*, March 2016, http://www.mckinsey.com/business-functions/organization/our-insights/Staying-one-step-ahead-at-Pixar-An-interview-with-Ed-Catmull?cid=digistrat-eml-alt-mkq-mck-oth-1603.

76. R. Sukumar, 'A Typical Job Interview is a Conversation between Two Liars: Fernandez-Araoz', *Live Mint*, 1 December 2014, http://www.livemint.com/Industry/D8cnH1YPxlNgAn81lxjPgL/A-typical-job-interview-is-a-conversation-between-two-liars.html.

77. Brent Weiss and Robert S. Feldman, 'Looking Good and Lying to Do It: Deception as an Impression Management Strategy in Job Interviews', *Journal of Applied Social Psychology*, 12 April 2006, http://dx.doi.org/10.1111/j.0021-9029.2006.00055.x.

78. Ron Friedman, *The Best Place to Work: The Art and Science of Creating an Extraordinary Workplace* (New York: TarcherPerigee, 2015).

79. Murray R. Barrick, Jonathan A. Shaffer, Sandra W. DeGrassi, 'What You See May Not Be What You Get: Relationships Among Self-Presentation Tactics and Ratings of Interview and Job Performance', *Journal of Applied Psychology*, November 2009, http://www.sitesbysarah.com/mbwp/Pubs/2009_Barrick_Shaffer_DeGrassi_JAP.pdf.

80. 'National Survey Finds College Doesn't Prepare Students for Job Search', Millenial Branding, 20 May 2014, http://millennialbranding.com/2014/multi-generational-job-search-study-2014/.

81. Marianne Bertrand, Sendhil Mullainathan, 'Are Emily and Greg More Employable than Lakisha and Jamal? A Field Experiment on Labor Market Discrimination', *The American Economic Review*, Vol. 94, No. 4, September 2004, pp. 991–101, https://www2.econ.iastate.edu/classes/econ321/orazem/bertrand_emily.pdf.

82. Curt Rice, 'How Blind Auditions Help Orchestras to Eliminate Gender Bias, *The Guardian*, 14 Oct 2013, https://www.theguardian.com/women-in-leadership/2013/oct/14/blind-auditions-orchestras-gender-bias.

83. Matt Mullenweg, 'The CEO of Automattic on Holding "Auditions" to Build a Strong Team', *Harvard Business Review*, April 2014, https://hbr.org/2014/04/the-ceo-of-automattic-on-holding-auditions-to-build-a-strong-team.

84. Steve Denning, 'The Joy of Work: Menlo Innovations', *Forbes*, 2 August 2016, https://www.forbes.com/sites/stevedenning/2016/08/02/the-joy-of-work-menlo-innovations/#2f2707d5cf86.

85. Kate Stanton, 'The Rise of the Middle-Aged Intern', BBC NEWS, 28 April 2016, http://www.bbc.com/news/business-36129892.

86. Tom Chivers, 'Could You Have Been a Code-breaker at Bletchley Park?' *The Telegraph*, 10 October 2014, http://www.telegraph.co.uk/history/world-war-two/11151478/Could-you-have-been-a-codebreaker-at-Bletchley-Park.html.

87. ibid.

88. Rich Hein, 'Acqui-Hire Trend Turns Startups into IT Talent Pools', *CIO*, 10 October 2012, http://www.cio.com/article/2391446/careers-staffing/acqui-hire-trend-turns-startups-into-it-talent-pools.html.

89. C.W. and A.J.K.D., 'Get a Life', *The Economist*, 24 September 2013, http://www.economist.com/blogs/freeexchange/2013/09/working-hours.

90. 'Founders IPO Letter', *Alphabet Investor Relations*, 2004, https://abc.xyz/investor/founders-letters/2004/ipo-letter.html.

91. Laszlo Bock, *Work Rules: Insights from Inside Google That Will Transform How You Live and Lead*, (New York: Twelve, 2015), pp. 136–137.

92. 'Staying One Step Ahead at Pixar: An Interview with Ed Catmull', *McKinsey Quarterly*, March 2016, http://www.mckinsey.com/business-functions/organization/our-insights/Staying-one-step-ahead-at-Pixar-An-interview-with-Ed-Catmull?cid=digistrat-eml-alt-mkq-mck-oth-1603.

93. Brian Williams, 'The Point of Pointless Corp.', Viget, 1 July 2009, https://www.viget.com/articles/the-point-of-pointless-corp.

94. Kaomi Goetz, 'How 3M Gave Everyone Days Off and Created an Innovation Dynamo', Fast Company, 1 Feb 2011. https://www.fastcompany.com/1663137/how-3m-gave-everyone-days-off-and-created-an-innovation-dynamo.

95. Aubrey C. Daniel, *Oops: 13 Management Practices that Waste Time and Money* (Atlanta: Performance Management Publications, 2009).

96. Dori Meinert, 'Is It Time to Put the Performance Review on a PIP?' *Society for Human Resource Management*, 1 April 2015, https://www.shrm.org/hr-today/news/hr-magazine/pages/0415-qualitative-performance-reviews.aspx.

97. Max Nisen, 'Why GE Had to Kill Its Annual Performance Reviews After More Than Three Decades', *QUARTZ*, 13 August 2015, https://qz.com/428813/ge-performance-review-strategy-shift/.

INDEX

ACKNOWLEDGEMENTS

Books like this one are rarely written with a skeleton of ideas already in place. They emerge, instead, from deep and often chaotic experimentation, coming together piece by piece till a coherent picture emerges. Also, it is rarely a solitary journey. Several people have worked with me over the last couple of years, playing material parts in the research at the foundation of this book. They have my deepest gratitude and include:

Sue Brooks and her community of business leaders at Imagine Talent. Sue, who I consider both a mentor and guardian angel, was instrumental in building belief and acceptance for the dynamic capability framework in this book. Her leadership ensured we could gather some of Europe's most successful organizations to play in the sandbox with us and prototype what future-ready management and leadership could look like.

Gale Ong, Armi Treñas, Christina Kimberly, David Stephenson and Sameer Miglani, who have proven themselves to be the faultless partners on all my research adventures across Asia, Europe and Africa. All the relentless toil, laughs shared and fun we had along the way have made the forty-odd assignments we undertook together seem like a seamless learning journey. For this, I am deeply grateful.

Jayapriya Vasudevan and Helen Mangham at Jacaranda, who do so much more for me than literary agents do. Pillars of strength would be as fitting a description.

My wife Nandini, who has been both an unshakeable pillar of support and the wind in my sails as I venture further and further into uncharted waters.

And finally, my two brilliant kids. Watching them grow into responsible and mature 'future talent' is what motivates me to think about tomorrow and stay curious about answers which lie just beyond the horizon.

ABOUT THE AUTHOR

Gyan Nagpal is an award-winning talent strategist and commentator who has deep expertise in researching ongoing changes to the global talent pool. Over the last fifteen years, he has helped some of the most ambitious international organizations build significant business franchises across the Asia Pacific and EMEA regions. He is the bestselling author of *Talent Economics: The Fine Line Between Winning and Losing the Global War for Talent.* He lives in Singapore with his wife and their two children.